Table of Conten

CHAPTER 1

Introduction

Do you walk on eggshells around your significant other? Are you tired of being told you are worthless and will not amount to anything? Tired of having no control of your own life? Tired of living in fear of angry out bursts, in public and in private? Are you tired of being blamed for everything in your relationship? Do you feel lost, helpless and jaded?

If you have answered yes to most of the questions, chances are, you are dealing with someone with a personality disorder. I am not an expert on this topic, but I have extensive experience dealing with narcissists, and would like to share what I have learnt over the years in the hope that it helps you to take the necessary action so that you can live your life how it is meant to be lived- with joy.

Creating this book is about increasing awareness about narcissists and helping those in a relationship with them. I understand the feeling of utter confusion, despair, and helplessness. Let this guide be the first step towards freedom.

I present this disorder to you in layman's terms so that even those without an in-depth understanding of psychological disorders will be able to follow. Also, I utilize information that has been borne out by rigorous research, as well as anecdotal stories of living, loving, and leaving a narcissist.

Narcissism is a complicated psychological disorder that has been portrayed pretty inaccurately in the media. This gives people a cartoonish idea of what someone with narcissism is like and may keep people from realizing the broad and wide-ranging ways in which narcissistic personality disorder can display itself.

Narcissism is a psychological disorder that has long been classified as such by the DSM, which is the main manual that mental health professionals use in the process of diagnosis. The DSM is the Diagnostic and Statistical Manual of Mental Disorders and is a means of classifying symptoms into different categories of disorder.

This manual provides the standard criteria upon which someone is diagnosed with a particular psychological disorder. It has a list of symptoms and other criteria that help determine whether or not a person falls outside the normal range for a certain type of behavior or thinking.

One of the problems with narcissism is that, it is an inherently toxic paradigm and the people who live with the narcissist are the ones that end up suffering the most and can, at times, unbeknownst to them, actually exacerbate the symptoms of narcissism.

I have real-life experience with this difficult issue as I grew up with a narcissistic parent. This relationship took me a long time to really figure out and come to terms with. Recovering from growing up with a narcissist is a lifelong process, I can tell you this from personal experience.

It is incredibly difficult to find out something so devastating about someone you love so deeply, and how their conditions make it so they cannot feel the way most of us do and must be treated with a lot of caution for my own sanity.

Another difficult thing about narcissism is that it can be tricky to truly diagnose except for in really clear-cut cases.

The thing is, a lot of the behaviors associated with narcissism are actually lauded as positive character traits, at least within certain fields. We don't often think about things in a more macro level, such as, while these traits may be beneficial to a stockbroker, the person's family is likely living in a toxic environment that does not provide a good indicator as to what a healthy relationship looks like.

Most narcissists are incredibly charming and it is often after we have found ourselves in a relationship with someone, or when we find the distance from a parent that is a narcissist, that we can see the problem lies with the individual.

There are actually quite a few fields – such as finance, politics, and business – where characteristics that, in regular life, would be seen as disadvantageous are actually a good thing. Traits like cold calculation and the ability to be cut throat without a second thought are thought to be important to success in certain, competitive fields, but when this type of behavior is expressed towards friends and family, it is not at all a good thing. So while we laud these traits, on one hand, they are highly detrimental on the other.

Another issue is that, especially when it comes to a romantic relationship, the narcissist often chooses people whose personality makes them more likely to endure the behavior of the narcissist.

They often chose partners that have had a history of abusive or neglectful relationships, they choose people who are isolated and don't have a strong support network.

In essence, they often choose their partners (or "victims" if you prefer) due to the fact that, by their very nature, they are going to be more prone to dealing with narcissism and its related effects without much complaint.

One of the most difficult things about dealing with a narcissist is that they tend to be incredibly smart and cunning and are highly adept at finding people who are likely to fall prey to their insidious charm.

A narcissist is often very good at courting people, both friends and lovers, with compliments, gifts, chivalrous treatment, easily sweeping people into their proverbial orbit.

People who have low self-esteem or a history of abuse or neglect are among those who are most vulnerable to a narcissist and the narcissist knows this, whether consciously or unconsciously.

They tend to be drawn to people who are co-dependent or that look for a strong, dominant male figure. However, it is certainly not unheard of for a highly intelligent and independent person to fall under the spell of a narcissist.

People who are used to abuse are much less likely to leave as a result of it and may lack the self-esteem to feel like they deserve any better. This ends up creating a cycle of abuse between the narcissist and the victim that is hard to break free from.

This guide is intended to help people understand the basic character traits, behavior, and personality makeup of the narcissistic individual. I present common red flags, survivor stories, and break down how to handle the narcissist in your life with as little damage to yourself as possible.

I touch on how to leave and recover from a narcissistic relationship, but this is something that is far easier to do with a romantic partner than in a parent-child relationship.

This is why I also devote a section of this guide to discussing the negative aspects of the narcissist parent and what this does to the child and how the child (or adult) can help protect themselves and break free of what can often be a dramatic struggle for independence and sense of self.

CHAPTER 2

Red Flags that You Are Dealing with a Narcissist

Being in any sort of relationship with a narcissist is going to be a roller coaster type affair and you are often going to be the one who pays the proverbial price. While it is often hard to pinpoint a narcissist when you first meet them, there are certain signs, or red flags, that you can watch out for that might indicate that you are dealing with a toxic person. The problem with these red flags is that they are often only obvious in hindsight.

As eluded to above, it can be difficult to really pin down a narcissist before it is too late. They often come across as highly intelligent, charming, genuine people – that is, until you are deep in a relationship with the person.

The other problem with these red flags is the type of people that a narcissist is likely to go after is someone who won't notice those red flags or be able to see them for what they are. As the narcissist is often a keen manipulator, people often don't realize what they've gotten themselves into before it is too late.

The narcissist seems like a prince or princess, treating you with immense grace and dignity, all the while, they are separating you from your support network and assuming more and more control over your life.

Many narcissists are highly adept actors and can even fake an emotional connection to suck someone into their proverbial web. It is this insidious nature of the disorder that makes it so hard to deal with.

Imagine meeting a man that you think is your Prince Charming. He sweeps you off your feet, promises you the moon, treats you like a princess, and then, well, then you find out what he's really like. Turns out, he's a manipulative and cruel individual that has a grandiose sense of self-worth and an inability to truly love and care for other people.

A lot of people found themselves in this unenviable situation – learning after marriage or even after having a child with such a person, that they are not what they thought. What makes this even worse is all the negative things that come along with any attempt to "fix" or leave the narcissist.

This is a nightmare situation that far too many people (both men and women) have found themselves in. While it is difficult to spot a narcissist at first, there are things to look out for that highly indicates this type of behavior.

If someone you know or love (or you yourself) display the behaviors listed below, it is possible that you're dealing with someone with narcissistic personality disorder. This does not mean that you should immediately leave the person, but there are some things that you need to know and expectations that need to be tempered if you hope to have a relationship with a narcissist without losing yourself in the process.

One of the problems with the narcissist is their ability to be like a chameleon. They can morph themselves into whatever they think you want them to be in order to get into your good graces, but it is never genuine.

The narcissist is often incapable of the normal range of human emotions, especially if they pertain to someone other than themselves. There is a wide range of ways that narcissism manifests itself, from the obvious to the subtle.

What follows are some of the most common red flags that the person you are dealing with may have narcissistic tendencies. These are, of course, not all the ways that narcissism can manifest itself, and these tendencies do not mean that those who have these traits are narcissists.

These are just common traits that appear more often than not in cases of narcissism and are among the most obvious red flags that can warn you to look into the person a little closer. All through this chapter I write 'Red Flag Observations' to make the picture clearer. If these statements are true for your case, then it is very likely you are dealing with a narcissist.

They make you feel insecure

This is not necessarily a universal trait of someone with narcissism, but it is a very commonly described feature of a relationship with a narcissistic individual. There are a lot of different ways that this behavior can present itself, but no matter how it is done, the purpose is to reduce their partner's sense of self-worth and dignity.

The narcissist will often say things that will undermine their partner's confidence and feelings of competency to the point where their partner begins to believe they are less worthy and competent than they really are. For example, your narcissistic partner bragging about their ex-lovers to you, frequently. Or how much they are in demand with the opposite sex.

This can be done in an overt or subtle manner, but the end result of breaking down self-esteem is the same.

For example, imagine yourself received a recognition at work for some accomplishment achieved. Then you come home to share the exciting news to your love, which happens to be a narcissistic partner. You tell your partner and they minimize it, maybe even poking fun at you for being proud of receiving recognition.

Perhaps they indicate that it is likely that other people who may have contributed to the project are more responsible for the recognition than you are.

However, their reaction towards you minimize your accomplishment to the point where you began to wonder if you even deserve it, or you may be convinced that you merely received recognition as a result of the hard work of someone else, or perhaps, you let yourself become convinced that the honor is trivial and without meaning.

Red Flag Observation:

They feel good by making you feel bad about yourself- your life, your decisions, your accomplishments etc. You are not sure if they love you.

They avoid emotional dialogue and closeness

One very common element of narcissistic personality disorder is not accepting the idea of being influenced or affected by the emotions of another person, or even their own emotions. They want to live life as a cold, calculating, and ultimately, a super-rational individual that is untouched and unsullied by unpredictable and irrational feelings.

The biggest red flag in my opinion is that your emotional needs are never provided for in your relationship with the narcissist.

Emotional outbursts are often met with ridicule and even cruelty from the narcissist and to them, it is a sign of weakness of character.

It threatens their sense of control over their lives and it can even be so extreme as to take the form of an inability or unwillingness to deal with the emotions of another person. It is easy to see how this can negatively impact a relationship and how hurtful and negative, psychologically, this can be to the narcissist's partner, friend, or child.

This can present itself in a variety of different ways. It might be that the narcissist deflects and changes the subjects anytime something emotionally charged is brought up. Or perhaps, they diminish your emotions and chastise you for being irrational in your actions and behavior.

Oftentimes, when pressed on an emotional issue or presented with an intense emotional outburst from someone else, they express anger, which is truly just a reaction to their inability to handle emotions – however, this is incredibly hurtful to the narcissist's partner as they feel demeaned and shut down.

Red Flag Observation:

They do not do any kind of soul-searching or self-reflection. Ever. They don't seem connected to their feelings or care about yours. Shallow, selfish and self-absorbed is an accurate way to describe them.

A broken family

It should be noted from the outset that just because someone comes from a history of abuse or fragmented family situation does not mean they will develop a mental disorder like narcissistic personality disorder.

There is a correlation, but not causation. What this means is that, when looking into the family background of many narcissists, you find a history of abuse and neglect, but not everyone that comes from a history of abuse or neglect end up being abusers and neglecters themselves.

This might seem self-evident, but for a variety of reasons, it is important to note that while there is a relationship between family history and narcissism, it is not causal or guaranteed.

It should also be noted that people who find themselves in relationships with a narcissistic individual are more likely to come from an abusive or neglectful background.

The thing is, a narcissist is incredibly good at deception and can actually make up a family sob story as a means to hook a partner via sympathy. If the back-story of the person doesn't quite make sense, you should keep an eye out for other indicators that the person might not be what they seem.

Red Flag Observation:

They have had an unhappy or unstable childhood.

Putting people on a pedestal

It might seem like the narcissist only thinks of themselves, and this is true to a large degree. However, many people with narcissism will look up to an almost cultish degree, to certain celebrities or authority figures.

They are also likely to put people up on a pedestal, such as those they are in a relationship with. While this might seem like they are treating their partners with an incredible degree of reverence and respect, it actually indicates something far more sinister.

When they put their partner, their child, or a friend up on a proverbial pedestal, what this ends up meaning is that this person will be held to a higher standard than anyone else. This means that the person is seen more as a cartoonish image of what the narcissist wants them to be like, than what they actually are like.

People who find themselves in a relationship with someone like this often find that, it is almost impossible to reach the standards set for them by their partner.

Disappointment, when you fail to live up to their ridiculous image of what you should be like, is often heaped on with abuse, guilt, and shaming. Calling you names, verbal abuse and devaluing you is a common example.

Making a mistake and not living up to the image the narcissist has of you can lead to outbursts of anger and abuse – both verbal and physical. A common trait from a narcissist after an outburst is indignation, as well a high degree of flattery to get you back on their good side.

Red Flag Observation:

In the beginning of the relationship, they worshiped the ground you walked on.

Incredible need for control

As been indicated in other sections of this guide, control is a huge issue for people who have narcissistic personality disorder. This helps to explain why the narcissist has such a negative reaction to emotions, both their own and the emotions of others.

When faced with emotions, they feel like their ability to control the situation has become compromised and this leads to feelings of anxiety and can result in outbursts of anger. A lack of control makes the narcissist feel vulnerable, which is one of the worst things for them to feel.

A narcissist is not likely to be the type of person to ask for things and let someone else lead the way. They will want their children, friends, and partners to follow them and allow them to dictate every element of life. How you dress, who you meet, when you meet them and most importantly how you think- will be controlled by the narcissist.

Any attempts on the part of a loved one to exert any sort of control can lead to vitriol and anger that is far in excess of what is called for in the said situation. Disproportionate anger is a huge red flag.

The narcissist is a huge planner. They want to plan for every possible detail and outcome, as they do not want to be blindsided by something they failed to think of and plan for.

This often extends to every area of their life. They will want to control all elements of their life, including the people in it. This can lead to manipulative, controlling, and abusive behavior if their loved one tries to exert any control over their situation or life.

In those events where the narcissist has no choice but to rely on someone else, they often accept this help with anger.

For those in a relationship with a narcissist, who has a strong need for control often censor their own behavior so as not to upset the narcissist in their life. Making choices, to a partner or child of a narcissist, often doesn't seem like an option. The idea that they can modify or disobey plans never comes to their mind.

This is why the narcissist often tries to alienate their partner or children from their social circle, as it allows them to exert more control over the person.

Red Flag Observation:

You are told what to do, in every area of your life.

An inability to take criticism or negative responsibility.

Narcissists tend to put themselves on a pedestal, valuing their own opinions, intellect, and judgment over anyone, no matter how capable. These people are experts at everything and cannot be taught anything.

They tend to talk at, not to the people around them, more given to monologues than actual conversation. They do not take criticism well and will often respond excessively even to the most mild criticism.

The narcissist is also not one that is likely to take responsibility for anything that goes wrong. Negative things are always someone else's fault, whereas anything positive is the result of the narcissist and the narcissist alone.

Red Flag Observation:

They assume no accountability of their wrongdoing. It is either your fault or someone else's. Always.

Grandiose sense of self.

Perhaps the most commonly understood manifestation of narcissism is the excessive and overinflated sense of self. To the narcissist, they are at the top of the proverbial food chain. They likely see themselves as some sort of oracle or prophet, "blessing" the world with their knowledge and their presence. This incredible level of self-confidence is also what often makes the narcissist a success in their careers, but it also makes them frustrating individuals that cannot really have normal relationships with other people.

Red Flag Observation:

Their motto is I, me and myself. They put themselves first. A favorable public image is of the utmost importance to them.

Unreasonably critical of those closest to them.

Ask the child of a narcissist and a common refrain you are likely to hear is that there was nothing the child could ever do that was good enough for their narcissistic parent.

They often hold their friends and family to a higher standard of conduct and success than they even ask of themselves. Failing to meet these unreasonable standards is often met with criticism, blame, and even guilt.

Red Flag Observation:

They never miss an opportunity to disparage others. They are habitual faultfinders and are suspicious of everyone's motives.

Pathological liars

A narcissist lies with ease and without any shame or guilt. They twist and turn facts to suit them; suit their perception of reality. In their head these lies make perfect sense as they fit well in their false narrative of being a hero or a victim.

Red Flag Observation:

They lie.

CHAPTER 3

Types of Narcissists

Depending on whom you ask, there are quite a few different types of narcissists. These different types all share some common characteristics, but there are differences in how their narcissism is displayed in terms of behavior, thought, and action.

For the sake of simplicity, here will cover the five most common types of narcissism and dive into the inner workings and common behaviors associated with each type.

This list is, of course, by no means exhaustive. I do, however, include the most common types that are found on most lists of different types of narcissistic personality disorder.

Like many disorders, like depression and autism, narcissism can be seen as a spectrum of disorders. This means that some people can have a more severe or mild form of the disorder and this will effect how this disorder will manifest itself. Some types are easier to treat and easier to live with than others.

If you live or love someone you suspect of being a narcissist, read on to find out details of the different types of narcissism and how they present themselves. Those who have a very mild case of narcissism might actually be highly successful and productive members of society. Some people who suffer from narcissism are otherwise healthy people, with a slightly inflated sense of self. So it cannot be said that just having a narcissistic tendency makes one a narcissist.

Also, like many disorders, television, movies, and the media have painted a pretty narrow and not entirely accurate picture of what a narcissist is like. The problem with this is that it gives people a false impression of what this disorder is really like, which leads many people to assume that the person they suspected to be a narcissist isn't because they don't display "x" symptom.

Just like there are endless types of people, there are tons of different ways that narcissism can express itself.

Before I dive into the different types, we should also note that there aren't really any widely used labels for these different types, even though they do tend to refer to the same type of case. I have used the most descriptive label that is in common use for each type as it makes it easier to distinguish by the title alone.

Mr. or Ms. Know-it-all

Again, while having a tendency to feel like you have an expert opinion on everything can be indicative of narcissism, it is not directly correlated. With narcissists, you often see the whole know-it-all phenomena played out to an extreme degree.

A know-it-all narcissist is one of those people who always have an opinion on something, one that isn't up for debate, and that often is not solicited to begin with. This type of narcissist can seem combative and they often dominate any conversation where an "expert" opinion might be helpful.

This type of narcissist will be the type of lecture. They engage in monologues, not dialogues. Rather than listening to what other people are saying, they are often busy thinking about what they would say next. And if anyone dares to disagree with a know-it-all narcissist, there is likely to be an outburst of indignation and anger to follow.

They may or may not be an expert in the field they are giving their opinion on, but any questioning of their authority to discuss such as topic is likely to be met with vitriol.

It can be difficult to deal with a person with this type of narcissism as nothing ever gets through to them. They either aren't listening or won't let anyone else get a word in edgewise.

If you are in a situation where you must interact with someone who is this type of narcissist, it is helpful, if possible, to ignore the litany of suggestions and advice that they throw your way. Know that if you challenge their expertise or judgment, conflict is the likely response. If they demand a response, try to be open without explicitly agreeing with their viewpoint.

The God complex.

This is probably the more "textbook" type of narcissist most people are familiar with, as this is often the type we see portrayed in books, movies, and television. The reason we see this type of narcissist portrayed so often in Hollywood is that this is the so-called "sexy" type of the disorder that is marked by a grandiose sense of self-worth importance.

These individuals are often incredibly charming, even though they care about nothing beyond themselves. Some with this type of narcissism feel like they are better or superior to everyone around them, including their friends and family.

They often feel like they are destined for greatness and if they do not achieve said greatness, it is the result of circumstances and other people in their life that held them back. This type of narcissist will never accept personal responsibility for any of their failures or mistakes, they will always pin the fault on someone else and they truly believe this to their core.

It is almost as if they have an inability to be at fault for anything and it is unfathomable that something that goes wrong could be the fault of anyone but them.

Another reason this type of narcissism tends to be romanticized in a film is that people with this type of narcissism are often, as noted above, very charismatic and affable. They are also often incredibly successful in their personal and professional life, in part due to their incredibly high sense of self-esteem.

This type of individual will never let you forget any accomplishment they achieve and they may feel personally threatened if a friend or family member experiences their own success, they may even demean the success of the other person. This type of person will drop people, even those that are close to them, if they perceive them as a liability or impinging on their success, and they are not the kind of people you can rely on in a time of need, regardless of how genuine they might seem.

It is easy to be drawn to this type of person as they seem to have it all together and other people seem to flock to them as if they might have the same type of success and confidence by merely being in the orbit of said individual.

This person is always tooting their own proverbial horn and some people immediately see through it, whereas others find themselves drawn to it.

It can be natural to want to stand up to some with this type of narcissism, as it feels like you are constantly being undermined and are under attack, nothing you do is ever good enough for the narcissist with the over-inflated sense of self.

However, the problem with challenging someone with grandiose narcissism is that you often end up further entrenching the individual in their sense of superiority. Challenging the narcissist might lead to confrontation and conflict.

You shouldn't expect them to either understand or be grateful that you showed them the error of their ways. At best, they will ignore you, and at worst, this can trigger a lot of drama.

Complimentary narcissists

This is a less common type of narcissism, but it is actually one of the more dangerous and insidious types of narcissism we will discuss in this guide.

What makes this kind of narcissist different from the other types we have described is their means of manipulating those around them. Rather than dominating their friends and loved ones with their superiority and outward need for control, these individuals ingratiate themselves to people by making them feel good about themselves. This might not seem like a bad thing at all, but it is a means to an end that has a lot of negative ramifications.

Basically, what this type of narcissist is known to do is worship the very ground you walk on.

At first, they will charm you with chivalry and admiration. They are likely to shower you with compliments over how amazing, smart, beautiful/handsome, etc., you are. And naturally, people are drawn to this because we like to hear nice things about ourselves and it is good for our confidence and self-esteem.

However, with the narcissist, this is not genuine. It is how they develop a relationship with someone before they show their true colors. One major indicator is that they say, "I love you" very early on in the relationship.

Just like the textbook narcissist, we see on film and television screens, this type of narcissist is often incredibly charming, affable, funny, and seemingly kind and genuine. However, this is an act that falls away once the individual has you in a committed relationship with them.

What is interesting is that, most people don't see how they are being used in this type of relationship, as their partner seems to just say wonderful things that make their partners feel loved, competent, and happy.

Really, what happens is that this type of narcissist will actually use compliments and nice treatment as a way to manipulate you into doing what they want. Once they are ingratiated to you, you are more likely to do what they want.

If they do something wrong, and then shower you with compliments and praise, you are much more likely to forgive and forget, which is exactly what they want.

A lot of people never realize they are with a narcissist like this until they fail to come through on what the person wanted them to do, or they get dropped because they are no longer useful to the narcissistic individual.

One way to avoid falling prey to this type of narcissist is to stay humble.

While it is nice to hear wonderful things about yourself, excessive flattery is very rarely genuine. It is always used as a means to an end and it should be a huge red flag.

Another way to ferret out this type of narcissist is to see how they act to people that don't provide any utility to them. How do they treat wait staff or random people on the street? What about people they dislike?

If you see a huge disparity in how they treat you versus how they treat everyone else, you might want to pay closer attention to their behavior for other signs indicating that they are a complimentary narcissist.

The bully

There are some types of narcissism that are nothing but toxic. While the other types of narcissism often present themselves in the way of charming, charismatic, yet manipulative behavior, the bully is a different animal completely.

This type of narcissist is incredibly hurtful. They can only feel good about themselves at the expense of other people. They spend a lot of time expressing superiority over other people, as well as contempt for anyone who dares to challenge or disagree with them.

This type of narcissist is similar to the know-it-all or the narcissist with the over-inflated sense of self in that they feel an innate and overriding superiority over pretty much everyone around them.

The real difference is in how these feelings manifest themselves. The bully isn't satisfied with "winning," they only feel good when they can cut down others for their failure, rather than holding up their own success. This type of narcissist is a classic bully.

They are often cruel in their treatment of anyone around them, even people they claim to love or who are there to help them.

They are often violent, at least emotionally, and in the event they need something from you, they do not approach from a humble approach, they tend to use threats to get what they want.

People in close relationships with this type of narcissist often find themselves with little to no self-esteem or feelings of self-worth. The bully not only seeks to belittle your accomplishments, but they also want you to doubt your value to humanity and to feel like they are doing you a favor by being a friend or lover.

This type of narcissist is incredibly hard to live with as you can start to feel beat down or resentful of constant verbal abuse. You have to be careful how you deal with this kind of narcissist, as the bully is just a few steps away from being an actual physical abuser.

I discuss how to avoid riling up the narcissist, as well as how to live and leave the various types of narcissists in the sections that follow.

The grudge holder

Another incredibly dangerous and insidious type of narcissistic personality disorder is the vindictive narcissist.

In many ways, this type of narcissist is dangerous to others in the same way that the bully can be. However, with the bully, you can avoid the rage and ire by simply not threatening their feelings of superiority and grandiose sense of self.

With the grudge holder, things are a bit different.

Say you challenge, even in some seemingly innocuous way, someone who is a vindictive narcissist. Perhaps you disagreed with their point of view on something at work.

For most people, this would be of very little consequence as people have healthy disagreements all the time. However, to the grudge-holding, vindictive narcissist, this is seen as a personal attack that has to be avenged in any way possible.

What starts as a minor disagreement, may turn into a lifetime of suffering for the poor individual who dared to take on the vindictive narcissist.

Once you are on the so-called bad side of the grudge-holding narcissist, there is little you can do to get out of their proverbial sights. They make it their mission, their purpose in life, to destroy you, as they feel that you have done them excessively wrong.

Generally, this starts off by way of spreading rumors and talking negatively about the person to co-workers, friends, or family members as an attempt to get the person's support network to turn against them.

This can be incredibly harmful. Take the example we mentioned earlier of the grudge-holding narcissist that you disagreed with at work. In an effort to get back at you, this person may not just spread rumors, but may actually attempt to get you in trouble by way of some sort of disciplinary action or even try to get you fired.

Suppose this vindictive narcissist is the parent of your children and you go through a nasty divorce. The narcissistic parent may use this perceived slight as an excuse to turn your own children against you.

This often leads to unnecessarily strained relationships and years fighting things out in the court system – none of this helps anyone except the vindictive narcissist feels as if they have exacted some sort of revenge.

Due to the very nature of the type of narcissist the grudge holder is, it can be very difficult to successfully navigate a relationship with the person, especially if they feel like you are a threat to them or that you may challenge their superiority.

If you can suss out that this person has a history of grudge holding behavior, it might be best to hold your tongue as what they end up putting you through is not worth it.

This might not seem fair, or it might seem like this is letting the "bad guy" win, but these people are often highly motivated by their vindictiveness and you and your family can really end up suffering as a result.

As we noted at the opening of this section, this is not a complete list of different types of narcissism, but these are the most common and a lot of the other types could easily be placed in a subcategory of one of the types we describe here.

It is probably a lot easier to see now how there truly a pretty broad spectrum of how severe or mild narcissism can be and how it manifests itself in terms of outward behavior.

Some types are easier to cope with than others and there are forms, such as the bully or the vindictive narcissist that are pretty much all around toxic, that need to be handled with caution.

In the following sections, we will discuss the two main ways that narcissistic behavior tends to present itself, either overtly or covertly. Whether narcissistic tendencies are subtle or obvious might not seem like a very important distinction, it actually is.

Depending on the type of narcissism you are dealing with and whether it is obvious or subtle will help determine how best to handle, and removing yourself from said situation or learning how to cope if removing yourself is not an option.

CHAPTER 4

Overt and Covert Narcissism

As seen from the different types of narcissism, there are a lot of different and highly varied ways that this type of behavior presents itself. Most commonly, we can distinguish this presentation in terms of overt and covert narcissism.

Basically, this can be said to describe the extent to which the narcissistic personality traits tend to be obvious or subtler. The overt, or obvious is a lot easier to identify, due to its very nature. Covert narcissism is a lot subtler and sometimes people who are victims of this type of narcissism have no clue as it is not obvious.

Overt narcissism

This type of narcissist is often the grandiose or know-it-all, who's feelings of importance and superiority are obvious from their behavior. They make no secret that they feel a great sense of self-importance and self-worth, and make no effort to hide the feelings of being superior to most people they come in contact with on a daily basis, including friends and family.

They tend to snub their nose at the idea of associating with unsuccessful people, almost as if they may become less successful just by way of being in the same room as someone they see as inferior.

The overt narcissist tends to have high feelings of entitlement and is the type of person who openly and aggressively deflects blame at all costs. For the overt narcissist, it is always the fault of someone else and they are unable and unwilling to take any personal responsibility, no matter how obvious their culpability is to everyone around them.

With the overt narcissist, there is no hiding their superiority complex or their disdain of people who they feel are beneath them.

We have all had an experience with the overt narcissist. These are people who can do no wrong, who are never to blame, who put themselves on a high pedestal and cannot be countered without aggression. This is the type of person that will try to make themselves feel superior by demeaning those around them. They point out every flaw that others have but never see their own. They are often arrogant, over-confident, and even cruel.

This type of narcissism can be displayed to varying degrees of severity, but we have all been in a situation with an insufferable, arrogant person who takes the utmost joy in cutting people down.

Covert narcissism

This type of narcissism is not only harder to spot and pinpoint, it is also more insidious than overt narcissism. The reason is that they work on such a subtle level of manipulation that most people don't see what the narcissist is doing. It can be very dangerous as they easily undermine their victim's self-esteem, feelings of self-worth, their accomplishments, and their value to society.

But they do this in such a way that it isn't obvious to the victim that they are being diminished.

While the covert narcissist doesn't have the level of arrogance and feelings of superiority that the overt narcissist has, they do tend to see themselves as the center of the world and their worldview is developed around that belief.

Since this type of narcissist doesn't see themselves as above everyone but does see themselves as the important "center" upon which their universe hinges, they tend to befriend people who are in worse straits or they feel are lesser.

For example, the covert narcissist may be more likely to surround themselves with people who have had fewer educational or occupational accomplishments as them, as a means to feel that, at least among their group of friends, they can feel some degree of success by comparison.

These narcissists do not appear to be as cruel as the overt narcissist, but their subtle nature can actually lead to some pretty bad results for anyone in the social orbit of said individual. The most clear-cut example of the danger of the covert narcissist comes in by way of the covert narcissist parent.

Since the covert narcissist doesn't feel that they are superior or have reached a pinnacle of success that might have been possible, they will often put their proverbial eggs in the basket of their children.

These are parents who ruthlessly push their children for academic or sporting success and are incredibly harsh and judgmental if the child fails to live up to the parent's ideal of success.

This often leads the victim to feel ashamed of their inability to please the narcissistic parent and the child pushing themselves even harder to reach an unattainable ideal. This sense of failure can often plague the child into adulthood and it isn't hard to see how hurtful and negative this is for a child.

CHAPTER 5

What Narcissists Look for
in A Romantic Partner

It might not seem like people who have a mental disorder would have a type, but it turns out that they actually do.

There are certain traits that the narcissist looks for in a partner, whether consciously or unconsciously, that makes them more amenable to the type of behavior that one deals with in a romantic relationship with a narcissist. Attractive (as it is good for their self-esteem), compassionate and people with empathy are mainly the targets.

As noted above, this may not even be intentional on the part of the narcissist, but the result is no less pernicious to the victim on the narcissist's "affections."

There are some more obvious things a narcissist looks for in a partner. They tend to be attracted to people who already have low levels of self-esteem and they have suffered from a history of neglect or abuse.

This is because people who have a history of abuse and neglect are already used to living in such an environment and they may be less likely or willing to extract themselves from the situation, as they may see it as normal, as this is the type of environment they've always lived in.

This is a sad turn of events for the victim as it guarantees them a life of shame and abuse from a partner that cannot feel for another person.

A widow is also very vulnerable to the charms of the narcissist, so it should come as no surprise that many narcissists develop relationships with people who have lost their spouse. These are individuals who are lost in the world and may not have had any romantic relationships outside of the one they had with the partner who passed. This means that they don't have a lot of real-world experience or negative experiences to keep them on high alert for potential red flags.

A lot of narcissists will manipulate the situation to where the widow gets to feel like they are playing the role of the savior of the narcissist – say from an evil ex – when they are really being played.

The narcissist is also attracted to people who do not or cannot have children. This might seem a bit strange at first, but look a bit deeper. One thing that is common to all types of narcissism is the constant need for attention, adoration, validation and so on.

When people have children, they tend to put their children first, which is a situation that a narcissist will have a lot of trouble dealing with, as they have the need to be the center of the proverbial universe.

People who don't or can't have kids don't have anyone to put ahead of the narcissist, making them just the type of person to give the narcissist the attention and environment they crave.

People who believe in more traditional values are also often a target of the narcissist. This mostly applies to narcissistic men looking for women. Women who believe that a woman's place is in the home and that the male should be the decision maker and head of household are much more likely to be willing to deal with the controlling nature of the narcissist. This arrangement is perfect for the narcissist as he will be able to make all the decisions and quickly squelch any dissent within the home.

Though this type of arrangement might be rarer nowadays than in the past, this is still an issue for women who want a traditional family arrangement.

It is often too late by the time they realize that they didn't marry a strong man, but a weak-minded one with an ego complex that is cruel and selfish.

Co-dependence is something that is incredibly common among partners of narcissists. What this means is that these individuals struggle with a separate personal identity outside that of their partner. They are likely to have trouble making decisions on their own and they come to rely on their partner for every aspect of their gratification.

It's not hard to see why this trait is attractive to the narcissist who is more than happy to assume control of their partner's life and love nothing more than being the center of their partner's universe.

Co-dependence is great for the narcissist but terrible for the co-dependent person. They will sacrifice themselves at the altar of their partner and the narcissist has no problem using them up and spitting them out when they've served their purpose.

CHAPTER 6

Living with a Narcissist

Love can be a really strange thing and it can cloud us to a lot of red flags and things that might not seem quite right about someone we are involved with.

I cannot tell you how many times I have heard stories about people who fell head over heels for someone, got married, had children, only to find out that this person was actually a selfish and cruel person who has no interest outside themselves.

Imagine having to come to terms with the fact that the mother of your children or your father is a narcissist and what all that entails in terms of your daily life.

This unpleasant situation is unfortunately, not as uncommon as you might think. Narcissists are dangerous because they are so good and successful at deception and manipulation.

These people know just what to say to get in your good graces and it is natural in the beginning stages of love to overlook warning signs or negative aspects of the person's personality.

The knee-jerk reaction to finding out someone who lives with a narcissist might be to leave, to move, but this just isn't feasible for a lot of people. If the narcissist in your life is your parent, you can't divorce them.

If the narcissist in your life is the father of your child, you still have to deal with him in your life. Whatever the case, there are a ton of reasons that people find themselves in relationships with narcissists that they cannot remove themselves from, so how do they deal with it?

Well, the answer is, there is no one answer. People cope with life's issues in a variety of ways. And it should be noted just how different a parent-child relationship is from a romantic relationship. This is why I tackle these two situations separately, as they cannot be dealt with in the same manner.

Parent-Child Narcissistic Relationships

One thing that both parent-child and romantic relationships with a narcissist have in common is the threat to self-esteem.

Finding out that you are married or in a committed relationship with a narcissist is often a bit of a slap in the face, so imagine how difficult it is to be the child of a narcissist and having to learn to come to grips with that.

In a lot of cases, it isn't until the child is removed from the situation, or they grow up and leave home, that they can start to gain some perspective about what they went through. When you live with a narcissist and it is all you have ever known, well, you don't know anything else so it is normal for you.

Being a child of a narcissist is a troubling situation to find yourself in and it requires a bit of a different perspective than being in a romantic relationship with a narcissist does.

When the narcissist is your parent, you have no control over this and there is nothing you can do to change this fact. The way you are brought up is often an environment that is not conducive to personal expression or thought and you likely have a lot of confidence issues that you struggle with.

The sad thing about the parent-child relationship when a narcissist is involved is that lasting and often irreparable damage is done to the psyche and self-confidence of the child.

A common experience of children of narcissist is the constant pressure to achieve the impossible. Failing to achieve this impossible thing leads to incredible disappointment and blame, even rebuke from the narcissistic parent. This can lead the parent to push the child even harder, or it can cause them to get angry and call their child a "lost cause."

In addition to the overachieving parenting style, there is also the common arrogant, and grandiose personality that manifests itself in nobody being able to live up to the perfection that is the narcissist.

Children of this type of narcissist learn to never question their authority, for fear of the rebuke and ramifications that can result. They learn that they can never match up. They are brought up to believe that the narcissistic parent is almost akin to a divinity.

It is easy to see how this is an unhealthy environment for a child and how it might take time to get over. One problem is that the child often has a difficult time letting go of their parent. This doesn't mean that children of narcissistic parents cannot have any sort of relationship with them, but you will need boundaries if you want the relationship to be healthy for all parties involved.

Too often, narcissistic parents just continue to manipulate their children into adulthood and beyond, never allowing their child to get out from under their clutches and influence.

Self-esteem, self-confidence, and learning how to make decisions about your own life are things that children of narcissists often struggle with. In a way, it can be seen a bit like living in a jail or military school environment. Getting out on your own, like going to college for example, often leaves these kids at a loss and unable to handle the pressures of determining their own affairs.

Covert and overtly narcissistic parents will often belittle and undermine their children. This leaves the child feeling inadequate and they have no value to society.

Low self-esteem and feelings of self-worth are commonly seen in children of narcissistic parents and can have a profoundly detrimental effect on their lives.

While incredibly difficult, once you have determined that your parent is a narcissist, you will want to find outside support networks and activities that will allow you to feel pride, to feel good enough, despite your parent.

It is important to know that their disorder is what makes them the way they are, but that they are wrong and the way you are treated is not right. This is often something that children of narcissists can only begin to do when they become adults and are able to physically and mentally separate themselves from the toxic environment.

It should be noted that no matter how good your outside support network, this kind of environment will have long-term effects.

Unfortunately, due to the nature of the parent-child relationship, there is only so much the child can do to inure themselves from the negative consequences of living with a narcissist.

Children of narcissists are the ultimate victims as they have no choice but to be at the whims of a selfish and sometimes cruel parent who is also the main authority figure in their life.

The best thing for the child of a narcissistic parent is for the other parent to remove themselves and the child from the relationship and environment.

Once the child is no longer in the narcissist's environment on a regular basis, parents and other caretakers can help repair any damage that may have been done to the child's psyche.

If you are the non-narcissistic parent of the child, you have a long road ahead of you once you leave the narcissist. You will have to work doubly hard to rebuild the child's self-confidence after years of not being good enough or never being able to compare.

They will need guidance on how to appropriately make decisions for themselves, and chances are, you will too. Your children, just like you, also need a strong support network of their peers, as well as adults, that can help them navigate life after a narcissist and help them become stronger, more independent and confident people.

Once the child has grown into an adult, they will have to learn how to best manage a relationship with a potentially toxic parent. This often means that the adult child has to set up certain boundaries to protect themselves and their feelings from the psychological hits that often come from being around a narcissist.

There are various strategies and even support groups for children of narcissist where people come together to share their experience, tips, and to just provide an outlet for one another.

Romantic Relationship with the Narcissist

Being in a romantic relationship with a narcissist is in some ways easier to deal with than being a child of a narcissist, and in some ways, it is also harder. This is especially true when there are children involved.

Any relationship with a narcissist is a complicated experience with tons of proverbial booby traps that constantly prey on the self-esteem and self-worth of the person living with a narcissist.

As I note in the section about parent-child relationships above, being able to protect your feelings of self-worth and self-confidence are incredibly important to being able to survive, mentally, a relationship with a narcissist.

If you're trying to stay with a narcissistic partner, you have to accept that this is not something you will ever be able to change about the person and you must be the ultimate decision maker as to whether you can overlook or forgive certain elements of your partner's personality.

There are certain things that you just have to accept if you wish to maintain a relationship with a narcissist. What follows are just a few scenarios that you are likely to face if you wish to stay in a relationship with someone who has narcissistic personality disorder.

A severe sensitivity to compliments directed at anyone but them.

As I mentioned earlier, the narcissist is very selfish and needs to feel as if they are at the center of the universe. Even minor compliments of someone else can feel like a threat to the narcissist and they may even blow up as a result in a way that far exceeds what is necessary or normal. You will have to learn to defuse these situations. They can get insanely jealous over the smallest thing.

Expect a one-sided relationship.

I'm not here to tell people whether or not their narcissistic spouse loves them or not, I am simply trying to explain what you should expect if you're trying to maintain a romantic relationship with a narcissist.

You have to accept that the relationship is going to be very one-sided.

Your narcissistic partner will expect you to look after them, to take care of them, to provide for them, but have no intention of acting in kind.

The fact is, your needs don't often even register in the mind of the narcissist.

Don't look to the narcissist for affirmation.

The narcissist will demand endless fealty from their partners by way of their constant need for attention and be the center of the proverbial universe. They will expect you to shower them with praises and to agree with their grandiose sense of self, or at least not deny it.

They tend to need constant coddling and are quick to resort to anger and aggression if they feel they are not getting their due when it comes to adulation. While they expect this from their partner, their partner cannot expect this in return.

The narcissist is not the type of person who will tell you that you've done a good job, that you look great, or anything of that nature. To the narcissist, the admission of the success of anyone else somehow takes away or undermines their own.

Don't expect them to care about the plight of others.

A lot of people naturally care about the people in the world around them. Many of us hurt when others hurt. We feel the pain of far-off people suffering from sickness or disaster.

This is normal human empathy that most of us easily understand and feel, but this is not the case with the narcissist. Not only do they not think about others, if they are tasked with thinking about others, they tend to dismiss these concerns as they have no direct bearing on the narcissist themselves.

You can bet though, that when a narcissist finds himself or herself in a situation of need, they most certainly expect the kindness and generosity they won't extend to others.

Don't expect to be able to connect on a personal level with a narcissist.

While they are adept at manipulating people into relationships, they do not actually have the emotional or personal connection that most of us have with our significant other.

The narcissist doesn't really feel the need to give a lot of personal details about themselves and is likely not particularly interested in your personal details either, though they often pretend to be at the beginning of a relationship as it suits them to do so.

In the beginning of the relationship, the narcissist will often dangle heavy threads of their childhood or personal life so as to seem vulnerable and open, but often these initial details (if even true) are the bulk of what you end up knowing about the person.

Become a good read of body language.

Unfortunately, a lot of the ways that you can cope with living with a narcissist require you to change and find ways to deal with the way that person is. This is not easy, of course, but it is possible.

One thing that can really help improve your home life if you live with a narcissist is to become an expert in their body language. People give off a lot of nonverbal cues as to their underlying emotional state.

Learn the signs of when your partner is getting agitated or angry, and try not to further escalate the situation. Save yourself a headache. It's a battle you cannot win. Save your energy for something more productive.

CHAPTER 7

Mistakes to Avoid When Dealing with a Narcissist

A narcissist is, in many ways, a lot like a bully, hence why one type of narcissist is regularly referred to as the bully.

This means that they can be nasty and persistent individuals who actually feed on cutting you down or exacting revenge due to some real or perceived slight.

Tangling with a narcissist often ends up badly for the person who tangles with them as they have an inability to see their own fault and if they feel like you slighted them, they are the type to make it their life's work to make your life miserable. These are people that you do need to exact caution when dealing with.

The thing is, you cannot think "normally" when dealing with a narcissist for the very fact that, well, they do not think normally.

You have to learn how the narcissist thinks and operates and keep this in mind at all times when dealing with one on a professional or personal level.

You cannot approach the narcissist on their level or expect a cooperative and team-oriented environment, this goes against the very nature of how a narcissist acts and operates.

You might also feel like you are the one person who can help the narcissist see the error of their ways and help them to reform their personality and behavior, so as to become more caring and a less selfish individual.

While this is a noble desire, it does not really take the reality of narcissism into account. Just like bipolar disorder or depression, narcissism is a mental health issue that cannot be "fixed" with compassion and hard work. There is a lot of evidence that point to this disorder being related to a chemical imbalance in the brain, just like many other psychological ailments.

This means that it isn't even necessarily possible for the narcissist to "snap out of it" even if they wanted to, which just isn't in the nature of the narcissistic personality to begin with.

You're setting yourself up for failure if you think you have what it takes to get someone "over" their narcissism. You might think you can convince them to seek professional help for this disorder, but narcissists are notoriously difficult to treat.

There are a few reasons for this, but the biggest one is that most don't see anything wrong with their outlook on life. Especially if the narcissist you are dealing with has achieved success in their professional life, you will have a hard time convincing them that there is something wrong with them, as they have achieved what many others only dream of.

They believe fully in their superiority and are likely to see attempts to help as direct threats or even a result of jealousy. Regardless, treating narcissists is unfortunately something that does not have a high degree of effectiveness. It's hard to get them to seek treatment to begin with, and if you get them to do that, they don't often follow their treatment protocol.

Try not to call out a narcissist directly.

A narcissist takes pretty much any perceived slight personally and not much gets under their skin worse than when someone they deem inferior dares to question their expertise or opinion. The narcissist can be incredibly arrogant and even vicious and it is natural to want to put this type of person in "their place."

The problem is, due to the nature of the narcissist's mental disorder, this often leads to abuse being heaped upon anyone who dares question the narcissist and if the situation in question is a work environment, you could lose your job.

Narcissists are often incredibly sensitive to criticism, perceived slights, or even outright condemnation. Their response can be defensive, and it can be vicious too. While it might be psychologically satisfying to go off on your ex that has put you through so much personal turmoil, it often doesn't end up being worth the blow back that you will likely face. It is fine to say these things among your friends, but if you directly challenge the narcissist, prepare for things to get ugly. They do not let these things go and hold a grudge, often for a lifetime. They will go to extreme lengths to turn mutual friends or even your own children against you in retaliation for daring to call them out.

It is frustrating not to be able to have that catharsis, but the narcissist is a dangerous type and it really isn't worth what can happen as a result. There are horror stories about divorces, child custody battles, and even work disruptions that result from a narcissist's ex daring to say something against them in a public or open type manner.

Don't appeal to their emotions.

The narcissist is often emotionless to an unhealthy degree and they often view emotions as irrational and beneath them. This means that if you try to appeal to the narcissist on the basis of emotion, they will see this as a sign of weakness and will either belittle and/or fail to understand the value or utility of your emotional argument.

Narcissist have very little respect or use for emotions and trying to use this as a means to change the narcissist's mind will only likely lead to angry outbursts.

Do not question their authority or control.

One of the fastest ways to make a narcissist mad is to challenge their authority or refuse to bow to their control. The need for a high degree of control is a common trait among all different kinds of narcissistic personality types. This can be highly frustrating and make it difficult to feel as if you have some semblance of control over your life.

One of the best pieces of advice for living with a narcissist is to not challenge their control, but also not to necessarily abide by it.

Chances are, your partner does not come with you every single place you go. They likely have a job and thus you do have private time without them present.

This means that you can use this time to do things your own way, without having to deal with the negative ramifications of going against the narcissist.

For example, a control freak narcissist may feel as though there is a "proper way" to do dishes and if you fail to follow their protocol, you catch a lot of flak. Let's say that you know that your way of doing it is just as effective if not more so. The best way to handle this is not to disagree with your partner when they tell you the "right way to do things," but rather, do it your own way when they aren't around. They aren't going to know the difference if the end result is clean dishes either way.

This is just a small way you can keep your dignity and sanity without setting your partner off on an outburst.

Maintain NO CONTACT.

This is something that obviously only applies to people who have been in a relationship with a narcissist that do not have children with the person.

If you don't have kids, the best way to leave a narcissist and to avoid any unpleasant happenings is to cleanly break off all communication and contact with the person and stick to it no matter what. The thing is, no matter how strong you feel – say some time has passed and you feel like you can handle yourself in an "amicable" discussion with your ex – they known how to manipulate you. The proof is in the fact that you were ever in a relationship with them to begin with.

When your narcissistic ex wants you back, they can seem incredibly earnest and contrite about how they treated you. They are likely to say all the right things, everything that you ever wanted to hear, just to get you back under their control.

Just the very fact that you left the narcissist is a direct challenge on their control over those around them and they are not likely to take this without a proverbial fight. They often ramp up the charm and may even play a victim role in order to get sympathy from you as a means of getting you back in their clutches.

Too often, this works, and we find ourselves back in a relationship with a toxic person, realizing our mistakes once we have been ensnared again.

This is why, no matter how sad they seem, how much you miss them, how good the past may seem, if you really want to do what is best for yourself in the long run, you need to stay strong and have no contact. None. Not through friends, not online.

No contact.

If they have a way to get in touch with you, they will always feel they have a chance and the narcissist is nothing if not confident in their ability to manipulate those close to them to get them to do what they want.

CHAPTER 8

Ending a Relationship
with A Narcissist

If you've made it this far into this guide and realize that you are in a relationship with a narcissist, you might feel pretty helpless, as if you are stuck with this person for the rest of your life, unless you want to be in constant battle.

Ending a relationship with a narcissist is a lot harder than it might seem. There are a lot of reasons for this, but one of the biggest is the type of people narcissists often chooses as their victims are people who are used to being controlled and mistreated. This often means that they don't often even contemplate the possibility of leaving the narcissist or having a life beyond them. But even these individuals often have a breaking point and at some point, are going to consider ways to leave.

Being in a relationship with a narcissist is draining and often comes at the expense of the other person's sense of self. However, due to the type of people that narcissists are often attracted to, people don't feel like they deserve better or that escape is really an option for them.

It is possible to extricate yourself from a relationship with a narcissist, but it is something that needs to be handled with care, as the narcissist does not take perceived rejection well at all.

What follows is some basic advice on how to leave a narcissist without getting their brunt of their hateful wrath.

Like any breakup, especially if you are married or children are involved, it requires a bit of thought and planning. Legal advice should be sought. Finances should be planned in advance.

Even if the split goes perfectly, it is still an emotionally charged time that is fraught with grief and even vindictive behavior. When the person you are leaving is a narcissist, these issues become an even bigger concern.

The problem is, the narcissist is controlling, vindictive, and knows how to manipulate you. They are often aggressive, quick to anger, and dogged in their pursuit for revenge over even the tiniest perceived slight. You really do have to keep these things in mind when trying to end a relationship with a narcissist, and try to make the process as painless as possible for yourself and your children, if you have any. Therefore, seek professional help!

First things first, if you are ending a relationship with a narcissist, you have to firmly and completely end it. This is not something that is feasible if you have children, but if you don't have kids, no contact is the first key to leave and stay away from a narcissist.

Narcissists are expert manipulators and know how to use people's emotions against them. Having contact with them after the breakup leaves you prone to verbal abuse or even a guilt trip that ends up with you back in that unpleasant situation.

You have to make a full and clean break.

If you need to get in contact with your ex for any reason, have a third party be your go-between and if they refuse to allow this, use the legal system to get the results you are looking for.

Do not under any circumstances allow the narcissist to use your things, pets, or anything else as a means of exerting control or influence over you. Leave getting these things back to other people who are apart from the situation.

The thing is, I cannot describe how important this rule is. The narcissist was able to manipulate you in the past and they know the tricks that work.

Expect them to try to get in contact with you and to use everything they have, including new tricks to manipulate you into coming back.

They'll reminisce about the good times, they will say those things you always wished they would when you were together, they may even court you again with gifts and lavish praise – but just remember that you cannot be swayed by these attempts as the person will revert to their selfish and controlling ways as soon as you are back in their clutches.

Next, you have to give yourself the time and support network you need to get over this relationship. A relationship with a narcissist is not like a normal relationship.

It takes a bigger psychological toll and can require a lot of rebuilding of self-esteem and also a lot of self-reflection to find out how you found yourself in the situation to begin with.

Do not try to ignore your emotions or chastise yourself for being lured in by a narcissist.

Surround yourself with friends and family that will help you build yourself back up after a fraught relationship with a narcissist. Let them be your rock and be your support network when you are struggling.

It is your support network that you need to turn to if you feel yourself caving or missing the "good old times." It is their job to remind you why you left and to keep you from falling back into an unhealthy relationship.

CHAPTER 9

Addicted to a Narcissist

This might not seem like a "thing," but you would be wrong. One of the most interesting phenomena about romantic relationships with narcissists is not the narcissist, but the person they are with.

This phenomenon is the seeming "addiction" that many partners of narcissists seem to have with their partner. There is still a lot unknown but a lot of psychological professionals think that this phenomenon is due to the very nature of the people who a narcissist is attracted to.

However, a lot of research still needs to be done to really understand why some people are addicted to someone they know is bad for them.

This odd phenomenon goes a long way in explaining why people in relationships with narcissists often have so much trouble letting them go and how easily they fall back into the clutches of their narcissistic partner.

A lot of this feeling of addiction to a narcissistic person often stems from the person's overarching feelings of helplessness.

They have never felt like they have control of their lives and being with a narcissist, who loves control, may have given them a sense of stability that they do not have on their own.

This is an illusion, as they are merely being used as a puppet to their partner's whims. But to someone who has never felt in control of their life, who feels helpless to make decisions, it is often more comforting to stay in an unhealthy relationship than to try to learn how to take control of their own life.

This is obviously rooted in deep-seated fear, but it is incredibly powerful and is often what draws people back to narcissistic partners again and again, even though they end up miserable and unhappy every time.

To people on the outside, it is hard to fathom what is going on in the mind of someone who cannot seem to quit a narcissist. The problem with this outsider's view is that they do not understand the complexity and subtlety of how a narcissist operates.

A narcissist has often successfully broken their partner down into a shell of their original self. They lack self-confidence, self-esteem, and even an identity outside that of being in a relationship with their narcissistic partner. To them, even though the relationship is painful, leaving involves leaving behind a huge part of their perceived identity, which is hard for anyone to do.

If you are part of a support network for someone who is trying to leave a narcissist, it is really imperative that you understand this phenomenon and act accordingly. It is easy to get frustrated with someone who cannot clearly see their situation as you, as an outsider can, but chastising someone is not helping them to get out of this unhealthy situation.

You need to be almost endlessly patient, as hard as this is, and try to have sympathy for the conflicting emotions that your loved one is displaying. This is all part of the process and if you really want to help your loved one break that hold the narcissist has over them, you have to be patient and willing to stay the course for the long haul.

In addition to feelings of helplessness and lack of control, and excessive sense of worry about the narcissist is also often a reason that people get trapped in a cycle whereby they cannot ever leave their narcissistic partner.

During the course of a relationship with a narcissist, you are likely to begin to feel as if your partner relies on you heavily for support. You worry about them and you feel responsible for them, even though you know that their behavior negatively affects you and that you aren't exactly happy.

This feeling of obligation and misplaced loyalty often leads the person back to the narcissist, even when they had the best intentions in mind.

Say, for example, you are really worried about your narcissistic ex and you call them up innocently just to check in on them and see how they are managing. How easily this innocent act plays into the proverbial hand of the narcissist. They are likely to use this as an opening to begin to worm themselves back into your life. Perhaps they tell you that they are not doing well without you at all. This will spurn your guilt even further.

At this point, chances are they already have you. The common way this ends up working out is that the narcissistic ex begins to court you again, remind you of all the good times, shower you with praise, and promise to be the person you always wanted them to be, and so on.

Then you go back...and months later you realize that you have been had but now it is harder than ever to leave. Not only have you reinforced this to your narcissistic partner, you are also indicating this to yourself.

This is almost like abandoning your own control over your ability to have a choice in the matter. While this is a choice, and it frustrates those who are trying to support the person leaving the narcissist, it does not feel like a choice to the person who feels this way. They feel trapped and as if they have no choice.

The "addiction" is reinforced every time you go through this cycle with your partner. Many people don't even realize they have something akin to addiction until they have tried and failed to really leave their narcissistic partners a few times.

It is a vicious cycle that feeds itself because it gives an even greater feeling of power and control over you in the mind of the narcissist, which means they will try even harder to maintain that control over you in the event that you ever attempt to leave again.

The only real way to break this cycle and beat the "addiction" is to cut off contact completely, and not restart it again at any point in time, no matter how many years have passed or how much someone claims they have changed.

CHAPTER 10

Rebuilding the Self After a Relationship with a Narcissist

Due to the amount of control a narcissist tends to have over our lives, a lot of people, understandably feel lost and a bit unsure of how to navigate their life after being with a narcissist.

That is, unfortunately, part of the control they have over us. They feed off our insecurity, how unsure we often feel, and then use that insecurity against us. These people often alienate us from anybody in our support network, to the point where the narcissist is all we have and their worldview dominates the proverbial conversation.

Control is something paramount to a narcissist and unfortunately, they often find themselves attracted to people who have low self-esteem, who feel like they have no control over their destiny. In some ways, it is the perfect combination – the narcissist needs to control and their victims often have no experience outside of being controlled.

The problem is, this is an unhealthy dynamic that reduces the victim to a shell of a person and often leaves them alone, with no self-confidence, and at a loss for how they should navigate the world.

The hardest thing about rebuilding your life after being with a narcissist is forgiving yourself for allowing it to happen. It is incredibly common for people to blame themselves.

They feel like they should have seen the red flags, or been stronger so they could have left earlier. All of these things are ways of deflecting the blame from where it belongs: on the narcissist.

A lot of highly intelligent people fall prey to this behavior due to the insidious nature of narcissism. It is not a character flaw to fall prey to a narcissist's charms.

Narcissists are keen manipulators and are great studies of how to get what they want from people. They are aware of what they are doing and often really, really good at it.

The types of people they prey on are chosen for a reason. Their victim is already in a low place and the narcissist swoops in and often acts like a knight in shining armor or offers to take control of the proverbial ship.

It also takes time to get over a toxic relationship like this. The recovery process goes far beyond not going back to the narcissist and forgiving yourself for being, well, human. These relationships do a lot of untold damage to people. They leave them jaded, unable to trust, perhaps even unwilling to attempt relationships again for fear of repeating the same experience.

While it is definitely important to give yourself time before you jump back into dating, you need to allow yourself to go through the stages of grief, but you also do not want to wallow in it. This is a good time to rebuild your support network, as this will be vital for you in the long-term.

It does need to be noted that, while you shouldn't blame yourself for ending up in a relationship with a narcissist, as well as having trouble getting out of said relationship, there are important lessons that need to be learned from your experience.

If you fail to look back critically on the relationship to see where the red flags were, where things took an unpleasant twist, and how, if at all, your personality enabled their control over you, it is likely that you will end up in a similarly unhappy relationship in the future.

This is not at all to blame the victim. That is what someone who has survived a relationship with a narcissist is: a victim. But there are lessons to be learned and there are things that you will need to look for and protect yourself against, so that you aren't a victim again and again.

The sad reality is that people who are often drawn to the narcissist end up with very similar partners throughout their lives, which is incredibly sad, as this is toxic to their very sense of self. Oftentimes, what these victims need is a support network that provides perspective and help to stay strong in the future.

It is okay to need other people, but it is not okay to let anyone control your life as the narcissist does. Having a broad coalition of friends and family will help keep you level, give you strength you need to make better relationship choices in the future. Also, to learn how to spot the signs that somebody is toxic before getting too deep with them.

One other thing that also needs to be touched upon is that, rebuilding process is difficult for people who have children with their narcissistic ex.

With children, complete disengagement from the narcissist isn't just usually an option. This makes the entire dynamic a lot more volatile and tricky to navigate. If you're in this situation, here are few things to help keep things as civil as possible, and keep the conversation to how best to support the children.

Though it is not ideal, but there are a lot of cases where it is best to have a neutral third party mediate between you and the narcissistic other. This way, they cannot manipulate you or pull any of the tricks used against you in the past. When there are mediators, things tend to be a lot more civil and respectful, as the exes are not speaking directly to each other.

If you feel that the narcissist is dangerous or unhealthy for the child to be around, bring this up in any sort of divorce or family court proceedings. This is the best time to air any concerns like this, as it allows for legally binding documentation of these concerns and special arrangements to be possible.

In a lot of cases, this is not necessary, but there have been horror stories about people who have tried to "play nice" with the narcissist and it didn't end well for them. The basic rule of thumb is to always be skeptical of motives with a narcissist, especially when your children are involved.

With children, things are always more complicated. That's just the nature of things. Even if your narcissistic ex isn't dangerous or particularly toxic to the child, their personality does require some level of explanation.

The child also has to learn how to heal and come to grips with the reality that one of their parents is a narcissist. Children of narcissists often need to have it explained that the situation is not their fault.

They probably need to have their self-esteem rebuilt. They may need to learn a variety of tactics that allow them to deal with their narcissistic parent in a way that doesn't cause the child undue hardship.

Regardless of whether you have children or not, rebuilding your life after being with a narcissist is not something that happens overnight.

It takes time, self-care, and a lot of reflection.

You need a strong support network that can be the shoulder you need to cry on as well as your rock in times of need. Your friends and family want to be this for you, all you have to do is let them. Your relationship with the narcissist may have alienated you from much of your social circle, but perhaps the best freedom after this kind of relationship, is to take back the control over your life and rebuild that circle stronger than it was before.

This is not something that happens overnight. A relationship with a narcissist can be a traumatizing experience. If you are the child of a narcissist, you may spend much of your adult life trying to come to terms with and get over your experience. You have to be patient and give yourself time.

There is no set rubric on how to heal or a set time frame on how long it should take you to "get over it." Anyone who is trying to push you along in your efforts to heal is doing a disservice to your needs.

A lot of people find solace in throwing themselves into their work, hobbies, or finding a cause they can get involved with. Especially right after the breakup, you don't want to be left with your own feelings as it is natural to start to look back, nostalgically, and forget why you left to begin with, especially if you are lonely.

Don't get yourself lonely or become preoccupied with the breakup. If you stay busy and don't wallow in the past, you will really help yourself along in the process of rebuilding your life.

Put yourself on a pedestal for a change. Being in a relationship with a narcissist means that your sense of self has taken a backseat to your partners. Once you have escaped, one of the most liberating things you can do to rebuild yourself stronger than before is to put yourself first for a change.

Focus on what you want, your feelings, your desires, your wishes. Look for ways that you can better care for yourself and ensure that you never let someone else take this away from you again.

Love has a way of blinding people to certain realities. This means we will often overlook red flags or things that should be really clear warning signs. We want to be loved, we want to be swept off our feet, and we want to believe that anyone who does this is genuine in their feelings.

Unfortunately, this is not the case for the narcissist. That is why I provided a long, detailed list of different behaviors that are some of the most common and obvious red flags that the person in question may be a narcissist.

People who attempt to leave a narcissist often find that if they don't cut off all contact, their narcissistic partner can coerce them into coming back through a wide range of means I described above.

They use common tactics such as guilt-tripping, promising change, and even showering you with gifts in hope of getting you back in their proverbial clutches.

The thing people find though is that, the narcissist quickly reverts to their old ways if you acquiesce, and this can also make it more difficult to try to leave again. This is why perhaps, the most important advice I can give to someone in a relationship with a narcissist that wants to leave is that you have to fully commit to no contact. This person will try anything and everything to get you back under their control.

Your leaving them is a direct threat to their ability to control the world around them, which can also lead them to act out against you in aggressive ways.

There is no shortage of stories about the horrors of trying to divorce a narcissist. They will drag their feet through the proverbial mud, they will try to rewrite history, they will try to take you for everything you have if for no other reason than that you had the nerve to leave them.

This is why I spend an entire section dedicated to things that you should avoid when dealing with a narcissist. Whether the narcissist in question is your boss, your parent, your partner, or soon-to-be-ex, these tips can help you make the process as easy on you as possible.

Rebuilding your life after being with a narcissist is a struggle and something that you should not rush or try to do on your own. The narcissist often breaks down their victims to the point that they are a shell of their former self. They have withdrawn, lost all self-esteem, no longer have an outside support network, and when they finally get the strength to leave, they are lost in the world. This is natural, but this doesn't mean that you should stay with the narcissist.

Finally, I conclude this guide with some advice on how to begin to rebuild yourself after you have successfully left a narcissistic partner, friend, or parent. It might seem like leaving the person is all that you need to get your life back on track, but the truth of the matter is that living and loving a narcissist takes a huge toll on your emotions and overall well-being. You need a strong support network to help you cope, heal, and move on from your experience.

With this support network, a clear head, and plenty of things to keep you busy, you have what it takes to break free from the narcissist in your life for good.

I hope this book has helped you get some clarity on why narcissists behave the way they do. Since this is not the be all and end all of narcissism books, continue your education by reading other great books on the subject that are out there. Thank you for spending your precious time with this book.

Remember, you are not alone and you are stronger than you think.

Printed in Great Britain
by Amazon

17712597R00032

Domino

TRUE HEROES
of
SPORT

OXFORD
UNIVERSITY PRESS

BEFORE READING

1 Match these words with the pictures. Use a dictionary to help you.

a ☐ baseball   **c** ☐ boxing   **e** ☐ Formula One   **f** ☐ skiing

b ☐ basketball   **d** ☐ cycling   car racing   **g** ☐ swimming

2 Look at the pictures and complete these sentences.

I'm good at . . .

I'm not good at . . .

I'd like to do . . . at school.

I like watching . . . on television.

My favourite sport is . . .

Pelé

EDSON ARANTES DO NASCIMENTO

Pelé helped to make football one of the **world's** favourite sports. He was born with the name Edson Arantes do Nascimento in Brazil, on October 23, 1940. His father was a football player, but in those days football players didn't get a lot of money. When Pelé was ten, he began to work, **cleaning** people's shoes in the street. On Saturdays he went to the football **stadium** and cleaned the shoes of people watching the **matches** there.

world people live in lots of different countries here

clean to stop something being dirty

stadium you can watch people playing sports here

match a game

One day Pelé said he wanted to be a **professional** football player. His mother was angry but Pelé said, 'Mother, I was born for football.'

professional doing a sport as a job for money

Pelé began playing football for a small **team** near his home, and when he was only sixteen, he went to play for the Santos Football Club. He got four **goals** in his first match. When he was seventeen years old, he played for the Brazilian team in the 1958 World Cup in Sweden. Brazil **won** the match with Sweden five goals to two (5–2). Pelé got two of these goals, and Brazil won the World Cup for the first time. Pelé played for Brazil, too, when they won the World Cup in Chile in 1962, and in Mexico in 1970. He is the only football player to win three World Cups.

team a number of people who play in a game

goal a point that a team gets in a game of football

win (*past* **won**) to be the best in a match

Pelé scoring in the World Cup, Sweden 1958

November 19, 1969, was a very important day for Pelé. There were 80,000 people in the stadium watching him play for Santos. They wanted to see him get his 1,000th goal. When he got the goal, he took off his famous number 10 shirt and put on a number 1,000 shirt. In all his 1,363 football matches, Pelé got 1,281 goals. That's nearly one goal in every match!

Pelé helped to stop a **war** for a time, too. In 1967 he played a football match in Lagos, in Nigeria. At that time there was a war in Nigeria, but the war stopped for 48 hours for everybody to watch Pelé playing football.

Pelé stopped playing professional football in Brazil in 1974. But today – all this time later – many people remember him and think he is one of the truly **great** footballers of all time. He called football 'the beautiful game' and he played truly beautiful football.

war fighting between countries and people

great important or good

Muhammad Ali

Muhammad Ali winning in 1964

CASSIUS MARCELLUS CLAY

Muhammad Ali was born with the name **Cassius** Marcellus Clay on January 17, 1942, in Kentucky. In the 1940s, things weren't easy for black people in Kentucky. Black people went to different shops from white people, and black children went to different schools from white children.

At school Cassius was more interested in sports than books. He was very good at boxing and **became** the Kentucky boxing champion six times before he left school.

After school, Cassius went to New York to learn to box professionally. His boxing was different. He moved quickly on his feet, and people loved that. In 1960, he went to the **Olympic Games** in Rome with the American team and he won a **gold medal**. A **reporter** from Russia asked him, 'In America things are bad for black people. How does it feel to win a gold medal for your country when you are black?' Cassius said, 'Some people in America are changing things.'

His greatest win came in 1964 when he became the World Heavyweight **Champion**. Soon after, Cassius became a **Muslim** and changed his name to Muhammad Ali. He wanted America to be a better country for black people.

Cassius /ˈkæsɪəs/

become (*past* **became**) to begin to be

Olympic Games games every four years between different countries

gold medal a yellow metal thing that the best sports people get

reporter a person who writes for a newspaper or speaks on the radio or television

champion the person who is the best at a sport

Muslim a person who follows the religion of Islam

The 1960s was a time when many Americans went off to the Vietnam War. Muhammad Ali thought the war in Vietnam was a bad thing, so in 1967, when they asked him to go, he said 'no'. Many important people in America were angry about this and Ali left the world of

Opening the Games at Atlanta, 1996

professional boxing for five years. Then he came back and became World Heavyweight Champion again for a second and third time.

Muhammad Ali was exciting to watch. He was a great boxer and always felt he could win – and he usually did! He often said, 'I am the greatest!'

In 1982, Muhammad Ali stopped boxing because he was very ill. In 1996, when he opened the Olympic Games in Atlanta, many people watching him on television were happy to see this famous sports **hero** from the past again.

Babe Ruth

GEORGE HERMAN RUTH

Babe Ruth was one of the greatest baseball players of all time. He was born on February 6, 1895, in **Baltimore**, Maryland. George's mother and father worked long hours

hero a person who does something important or good

Baltimore /ˈbɒltɪˌmɔːr/

and didn't have much time for him, so he played out in the street all day. When he was seven, he went to live at Saint Mary's, a school for boys. At first his parents took him home from time to time, but in the end he went to live at

Saint Mary's all the time. His parents never visited him there.

At Saint Mary's one of his teachers was Brother Mathias. Mathias became young George's friend and taught him to play baseball. George soon became a very good player. When he was

Babe Ruth with a young fan

only nineteen, he began playing professionally with the Baltimore Orioles. Because he was very young, the players in the team called him 'Babe' and after that 'Babe Ruth' became his name.

Babe played with different teams – the Boston Red Sox, the New York Yankees and the Boston Braves. He stayed with the Yankees for fourteen years, and his number 3 Yankees shirt became famous. In 1935 he stopped playing baseball.

Babe Ruth became famous and rich. He loved children and always helped them when he could. Over the years he gave lots of money to Saint Mary's school and to different children's hospitals.

In 1946 Ruth learned he had **cancer**. He went into hospital at once but the doctors couldn't stop the cancer. On April 27, 1947, he went to say goodbye to everybody at the Yankees stadium, but he was too ill to wear his number 3 shirt on that day.

Babe Ruth died the next year, but people didn't forget him. To this day April 27th is Babe Ruth Day for all baseball lovers in the USA and Japan.

cancer when you are ill with this, you can die

READING CHECK

Are these sentences true or false? Tick the boxes.

		True	False
a	Pelé's mother was happy he wanted to be a football player.	☐	☑
b	Brazil won the World Cup for the first time with Pelé in the team.	☐	☐
c	Muhammad Ali wanted America to be a better place for boxers.	☐	☐
d	Muhammad Ali didn't go to the war in Vietnam.	☐	☐
e	Babe Ruth learned to play baseball at home.	☐	☐
f	Babe Ruth helped children a lot when he was rich and famous.	☐	☐

WORD WORK

1   These words don't match the pictures. Correct them.

a   ~~stadium~~
   world

b   gold medal

c   reporter

d   world

e   goal

f   war

2   Use the words in the medal ribbon to complete the sentences on page 7.

become   cancer   great   match   team   1   professional   Olympic   champion   hero

a Muhammad Ali was the World Heavyweight boxing ...champion... three times.
I think he was a .... boxer.

b Muhammad Ali won a gold medal at the .... Games in Rome in 1960.

c Manchester United is a famous English football ....

d I'm not a .... footballer: I only play in my free time.

e I want to .... rich and famous when I'm older.

f When does the .... between Manchester United and Liverpool begin?

g Babe Ruth died of ....

h Babe Ruth was a .... for American children in the 1920s and 1930s.
He helped them and they loved him.

GUESS WHAT

Here are three people from the next chapter. Tick the boxes.

Who . . .	Jesse Owens	Cathy Freeman	Hassiba Boulmerka
a . . . came from America?	☐	☐	☐
b . . . made some teachers angry?	☐	☐	☐
c . . . ran for Australia?	☐	☐	☐
d . . . walked or ran to school?	☐	☐	☐
e . . . ran with no shoes on?	☐	☐	☐
f . . . won an Olympic gold medal?	☐	☐	☐

Jesse Owens

JAMES CLEVELAND OWENS

James Cleveland Owens was born, the youngest of ten children, on September 12, 1913, in Alabama in the south of the USA. He got the name 'Jesse' from the letters JC (James Cleveland) in his name. He was born nearly thirty years before Muhammad Ali, and things were worse for black Americans in those days.

Jesse was born to run. He was a very fast runner and he won all the **races** when he was at school. After leaving school, he went to Ohio State **University** to **train** to be an **athlete**. At university he lived in a house for black students only. When the athletics team visited different

race when people run and the fastest person wins

university people study here after they leave school

train to do a sport a lot to become good at it

athlete someone who is good at sport

towns in America, the white and black athletes stayed in different hotels, and once, when they all went out to a restaurant, only the white athletes got something to eat!

At the time of the 1936 Olympic Games, Jesse Owens was the fastest man in America. And he was one of the first black athletes to run for America at the Olympic Games. The 1936 Games were in Berlin, in Germany. Adolf Hitler was the **leader** of Germany at the time and he thought Germans were the best athletes of all.

Jesse Owens won four gold medals in Berlin and Hitler was very angry. He wanted the athletes from Germany to be the champions. When the time came for Hitler to give Jesse one of his gold medals, the German leader didn't smile or speak to him or give him his hand. He walked away angrily, because he didn't want to speak to a black champion, and he didn't want reporters taking photos of him talking to Owens.

After the Olympics, Jesse visited different towns in the USA and spoke about black American people. He thought black Americans were important people with a lot to give to the USA. He wanted to bring black and white Americans **together** through sport.

Cathy Freeman

CATHERINE ASTRID SALOME FREEMAN

Aborigines are black people from Australia. They lived in Australia thousands of years before white people arrived there from Europe. When the first Europeans arrived, they took Australia from the Aborigines. Cathy Freeman is the first Australian Aborigine to run for Australia.

leader the most important person

together with someone or near to someone

9

Cathy Freeman, Sydney 2000

Cathy was born on February 16, 1973, in Queensland, Australia. She was one of the fastest children at her school. When she ran, she **dreamt** of being in the Olympic Games and when she won a race, she dreamt of getting a gold medal.

Cathy's family didn't have much money when she was young, and they couldn't buy shoes for her to run in. Soon Cathy became famous. People called her 'the little Aborigine girl with no shoes'. When she was eight years old she ran for Queensland in an important race for young athletes. Before the race began, everyone laughed at Cathy with no shoes on her feet. But in the end Cathy won. After the race, she said, 'You don't need shoes to win a race.'

Cathy won her first gold medal in 1994 at the **Commonwealth Games** in New Zealand. After the race Cathy wore the Aboriginal **flag** and not the Australian one for all her photos. Many Australian people were angry about this. They said, 'Cathy must wear the Australian flag when she runs for Australia!'

But Cathy was a very good athlete and she went on running for Australia. In the end her dreams came true and she won her first Olympic medal at the Games in Atlanta. Then, at the 2000 Olympic Games in Sydney, she won a gold medal in the 400 metres. This time she wore the Australian flag *and* the Aboriginal flag for her photos after the race!

She says, 'You don't need money to win. To win, you must go after your dreams.'

dream (*past* **dreamt**) to think about something that you would like to happen; something nice but not true at the moment

Commonwealth Games games between more than fifty English-speaking countries that happen every four years

flag a piece of cloth with colours on it; every country has its flag

Hassiba Boulmerka

Hassiba Boulmerka is a person with dreams, too. Hassiba comes from Algeria, north Africa. In 1991, she was the first African woman to become a world champion. In 1992, she became the first Algerian to win an Olympic medal.

Hassiba was born on July 10, 1968. She lived in a village three kilometres from the nearest town. Every day she walked three kilometres to school and when she was late, she ran! She was often late, and running to school made Hassiba very strong and very fast. At school she won all the running races.

When she left school, she wanted to be a professional athlete. But in Algeria, some Muslim teachers think it is wrong for a woman to do sport and wear nothing on her legs. People in Algeria told Hassiba 'You must stop running!' but she didn't listen. She trained for eight hours every day. Her dream was to win a gold medal at the Olympic Games.

Hassiba Boulmerka, Barcelona 1992

Hassiba moved to Italy, and in 1991 she won the 1,500 metres in the World Championship in Tokyo. In 1992, she won a gold medal at the Olympic Games in Barcelona. It was a good day for Hassiba Boulmerka, and for Algerian sportswomen too.

READING CHECK

Choose the right words to finish the sentences.

a Jesse Owens was born . . .
    1 ☑ in Alabama in the south of the USA.
    2 ☐ after Muhammad Ali.

b Adolf Hitler . . .
    1 ☐ was happy when Owens won four gold medals.
    2 ☐ wanted German athletes to be the best at the 1936 Olympics.

c Cathy Freeman . . .
    1 ☐ is an Aborigine athlete from Australia.
    2 ☐ ran in the Olympics with no shoes on.

d Cathy Freeman . . .
    1 ☐ won Olympic medals for Australia in Atlanta and Sydney.
    2 ☐ thinks you need money to win a race.

e Hassiba Boulmerka . . .
    1 ☐ lived in a village in the country.
    2 ☐ wanted to be a teacher when she left school.

f Hassiba Boulmerka . . .
    1 ☐ left Algeria and went to live in Tokyo.
    2 ☐ won a gold medal in the Olympic Games in Barcelona.

WORD WORK

Find words in the British flag on page 12 to complete the sentences.

> I come from Britain. At the moment I am studying at Oxford **(a)** _University_ . When I leave I want to be a professional
> **(b)** .... , so I **(c)** .... for eight hours every day. Some of my friends and I go running **(d)** .... every morning. When I run in **(e)** .... here, I always win, and it's my
> **(f)** .... to win a gold medal in the Olympics. After winning, I'd like reporters to take photos of me wearing the British
> **(g)** ....

GUESS WHAT

The next chapter is about some famous young sports people. What are you going to read about? Tick four boxes.

Famous young sports people . . .

a ☐ . . . don't have any friends.

b ☐ . . . often go to live in a different country.

c ☐ . . . leave university because they must train a lot.

d ☐ . . . often leave the world of sport when they are older.

e ☐ . . . have reporters near them all the time, writing about everything they do wrong.

f ☐ . . . die young because they train all the time.

g ☐ . . . have an easier time when they are older and more famous.

Nadia Comaneci

Comaneci
/ˌkɒmæˈnetʃɪ/

gymnast a person who does gymnastics and trains to move beautifully

perfect with nothing wrong

Karolyi
/ˈkɑːrɔɪjɪ/

Nadia **Comaneci** was the first **gymnast** to get a **perfect** ten out of ten in gymnastics at the Olympics Games. And she was only fourteen when she did it.

Nadia was born in Romania on November 12, 1961. One day the Olympic gymnastics trainer, Bela **Karolyi**, saw Nadia playing at school. She moved beautifully. He thought, 'One day she's going to win a gold medal!'

Nadia began learning gymnastics with Bela Karolyi when she was six, and when she was eight years old she became Romania's best gymnast.

She became the best gymnast in the world on July 19, 1976, at the Olympic Games in Montreal, Canada. Many people went to Montreal that year to watch Olga Korbut, the famous young Russian gymnast. Nobody knew about little Nadia then. But she did very well. She didn't smile. She didn't do anything wrong. After she finished, everybody watching called out, 'Ten! Ten! Ten!' Nadia Comaneci got the first 'perfect ten' in the world of gymnastics.

Between 1976 and 1981 Nadia won eighteen gold medals. But in 1981, Karolyi, her trainer and now her best friend, went to live in America. Nadia wasn't very happy. She wanted to go to America too, because Romania wasn't an easy country to live in at that time.

One dark night in 1989, she said goodbye to her family and went to America. Today she lives in Oklahoma with her husband. She has a gymnastics school and teaches children there.

Jennifer Capriati

Jennifer Capriati was a winning athlete, too, when she was young. She was born in New York on March 29, 1976, and began playing tennis when she was three. At fourteen, she became the youngest player to win a match at Wimbledon. A year later, she **beat** the famous tennis champion, Martina Navratilova.

Jennifer Capriati, Barcelona 1992

In July 1992, at the **age** of sixteen, she won a gold medal for tennis at the Olympic Games in Barcelona, Spain.

But it isn't always easy to be famous when you're young. Jennifer had lots of reporters outside her house every day, and she began to eat a lot and became very fat. Then, one

day, someone saw her taking things from a shop. Soon after that, they found **drugs** in her bag. These stories were on radio and television across the world, and Jennifer felt very bad about them. In 1994 she stopped playing professional tennis.

But Jennifer **survived** these bad years. She wanted to get **healthy** and go back to tennis. She stopped taking drugs and eating badly, and began training. In 2001, she won the Australian Open Championship, and in June of that year, she won the French Open. 'Here I am again. This is my **second chance**,' she said happily to reporters this time.

drug something that people take to make them feel happy or excited

survive to live through a difficult time

healthy not ill

second chance a time when you can do something again

golf a game where you hit a ball into a number of holes

successful getting or doing what you want

soldier a person who fights for his or her country

Tiger Woods

ELDRICK TIGER WOODS

Tiger Woods was only two when he played **golf** on American television for the first time. No one knew this young boy was to become one of golf's most **successful** players.

Tiger was born on December 30, 1975, in Cypress, California. His father, Earl, is a black American and his mother is from Thailand. In the war in Vietnam, Earl Woods made friends with a Vietnamese **soldier** called Tiger. And so he gave the name Tiger to his son.

Earl loved golf, and often played it when Tiger was a boy. Young Tiger went with him, watched his father playing, and learned a lot from him. When he was eight, he became a young world champion. After that he won many golf championships for young people.

Tiger was very good at golf for his age. He went to Stanford University in 1994 and he was very good at golf there, too. After two years at university, Tiger left to become a professional golf player.

In 1997, at the age of twenty-one, Tiger was the youngest player to become an American golf champion. In 2000, he was the youngest golfer to win the four most important golf championships in the world in one year.

These days Tiger is rich and famous, and he lives in Florida because the weather there is always great for golf! He was the first black American to be successful at this 'white person's sport'. But when he was younger, some white golfers said he could not play with them because he was black. Perhaps his story can help today's young athletes to be tomorrow's champions.

READING CHECK

Correct the mistakes in these sentences.

fourteen

a Nadia Comaneci was ~~fifteen~~ when she got ten out of ten in gymnastics at the Olympics.

b Between 1976 and 1981 Nadia won eight gold medals.

c Jennifer Capriati began playing tennis when she was five.

d In 1984 she stopped playing professional tennis.

e In 2001 she came back, winning championships in New Zealand and France.

f Tiger Woods' father is a black American and his mother is from Vietnam.

g Now he is rich and famous, Tiger lives in California because the weather there is very good.

WORD WORK

1 Find nine words from Chapter 3 in the television.

2 Use the words from Activity 1 to complete the sentences.

a Athletes must dream of winning and work hard to be ..successful..

b Jennifer Capriati .... Martina Navratilova in 1991.

c At the .... of twenty-nine Nadia left Romania.

d Muhammad Ali didn't become a .... in Vietnam.

e Olga Korbut was a famous young Russian .... in the 1970s.

f When you get ten out of ten it's called 'a .... ten'.

g He was in a very bad accident but he isn't going to die, he's going to ....

h When athletes are training, they must eat .... things.

i Taking .... is bad for your body.

GUESS WHAT

**The next chapter is about sports people surviving bad times.
What are you going to read about? Make three sentences.**

a An American cyclist with cancer	**d** couldn't walk	**g** after a bad accident.
b An Austrian driver	**e** wins an important race	**h** after he gets better.
c An American runner	**f** doesn't leave his sport	**i** when she was a child.

Lance Armstrong

pool a building where you can swim

Lance Armstrong was born in Plano, in Texas, on September 18, 1971. Plano is famous for American football, but Lance was good at running. When he was at school he entered a running race. Before the race, Lance's mother gave him a 1972 dollar and said, 'This is to help you win.' Lance won the race.

At the age of twelve, Lance learned to swim. He loved it, and began to train every day. To get to the **pool**, Lance cycled. Every day, he cycled sixteen kilometres to the pool, swam for ten kilometres, and then cycled sixteen kilometres back home.

After he left school, he began cycling professionally. He went to live in Europe and dreamt of cycling in the Tour de France, the most famous cycle race of all.

Lance Armstrong, Tour de France 2000

By 1996, Lance Armstrong was the best cyclist in the world. But he left the Tour de France that year because he felt tired and ill, and he went back to America to see a doctor. Lance had cancer and he had it badly, but he said, 'I'm going to survive and I'm going to cycle again one day.'

After some time in hospital, Lance and the doctors beat the cancer and he got well again. Soon he began to think about going back to cycling. In 1999, and again in 2000, Lance won the Tour de France. When he cycled through Paris at the end of the race he was happy to win, and to be alive. In 2001, he won the Tour de France for the third time.

Niki Lauda

ANDREAS NIKOLAUS LAUDA

Niki **Lauda** was born in Vienna, Austria, on February 22, 1949. He was always very interested in cars and racing. Car racing is an expensive sport, but Niki came from a rich family. He became a professional racing driver in 1971 and dreamt of being a Formula One driver.

One day Niki met Luca **Montezemolo** from Ferrari. Montezemolo thought Lauda was a good driver and asked him to race for Ferrari. Niki won his first race for Ferrari in 1974, and a year later, he won the Formula One World Championship.

But Niki Lauda is most famous for losing the Championship in 1976. Niki began the German race in front of everyone. After a short time his car suddenly went off the road. It was **on fire**. Three drivers stopped and helped get Niki out of his car.

Lauda /ˈlaʊdə/

Montezemolo /ˌmɒnteˈzemɒlɒ/

on fire   red, hot and burning

He had very bad **burns** all over his body, and he was very ill. The doctors at the hospital said, 'We're afraid he's dying.' But after some days Niki opened his eyes and said, 'I want to go back and finish the Championship!'

Six weeks later Niki was back. He was in front of all the **other** drivers in the earlier races and he knew he could win the championship. The last race was in Japan. On the day of the race there was a lot of rain and Niki couldn't see the road in front of him. He thought it was very **dangerous** to drive that day, so he left the race. In the end he lost the championship.

Niki won the Championship in 1977. In 1979 he stopped racing but went back for a short time in the 1980s and won the 1984 World Championship. People remember Niki Lauda today because he survived a bad accident and went back soon after to race again.

burn you get this on your body when you are in a fire

other different

dangerous that can kill you

Wilma Rudolph

Wilma Rudolph was the first black American woman to win three gold medals at the Olympic Games. She was born on June 23, 1940, in Clarkesville, Tennessee, and had twenty-one brothers and sisters. At the age of four, she was very ill. She couldn't go to the hospital in Clarkesville because it was only for white people. When the only black doctor in Clarkesville saw Wilma's legs he said, 'This little girl is never going to walk again.'

Wilma's mother didn't listen. Every day she worked on Wilma's legs with her hands. When Wilma was six, she moved about the kitchen on one leg for the first time.

Then, when she was twelve, Wilma began to walk again and could go to school. There she began playing basketball and was very fast on her legs. In 1957, she went to Tennessee State University and trained to be a runner.

In 1960, Wilma went to Rome for the Olympic Games. She won three gold medals there – in the 100 metres, the 200 metres, and the 4x100 metres **relay**. The reporters called her 'the world's fastest women'.

When Wilma came home to Clarkesville there was a big **party** for her. White people came out on the streets with black people to say 'hello' and 'thank you' to Wilma. Later Wilma became a school teacher and helped black and white children train to be athletes. She died in 1994. In Tennessee, June 23rd is now called Wilma Rudolph Day.

relay a race for a team of four runners

party a meeting of people to eat, drink and be happy

23

READING CHECK

Are these sentences about Lance Armstrong, Niki Lauda, or Wilma Rudolph? Tick the boxes.

This person . . .	Lance Armstrong	Niki Lauda	Wilma Rudolph
a . . . was very ill and couldn't go to school.	☐	☐	☑
b . . . was good at running and swimming.	☐	☐	☐
c . . . had a bad accident in a race.	☐	☐	☐
d . . . left a race because it was raining.	☐	☐	☐
e . . . felt very ill and left a race.	☐	☐	☐
f . . . came from a rich family.	☐	☐	☐
g . . . came from a very big family.	☐	☐	☐
h . . . started training at university.	☐	☐	☐

WORD WORK

Find words from Chapter 4 to complete these sentences.

a Help! My car is on ....fire........ !

b Oh no! I can't win any medals with these .... on my hand.

c We all had a good time at the
.... after the Games.

d Boxing can be a .... sport.

e I don't have to go far to train – there is a
swimming .... in our garden.

f Hurry up Wilma! We can't win the
.... without you.

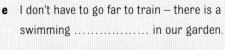

GUESS WHAT

The next chapter is called 'Perfect bodies?'
What are you going to read about? Tick four boxes.

a ☐ A doctor tells a child to go swimming when she is ill.

b ☐ A famous swimmer has cancer.

c ☐ A famous basketball player learns he is badly ill when he is thirty-two.

d ☐ A basketball player has one arm.

e ☐ A sportsman loses his leg after an accident in Australia.

f ☐ A sportsman has five legs.

Amy Van Dyken

The swimmer Amy Van Dyken is the first American woman to win four gold medals in one year at the Olympic Games. Her gold medals at the 1996 Games in Atlanta are all the more wonderful because Amy has very bad **asthma**. Because she has asthma she can't **breathe** very well. Swimmers without asthma can breathe 35% better than Amy can.

Amy was born in Colorado on February 15, 1973. The other children at her school didn't want to play with her because she couldn't run very well. They laughed at her and they called her a '**nerd**'.

Amy began swimming at the age of six when her doctor told her, 'Perhaps swimming can help you breathe more easily.' It was hard work for Amy and she couldn't swim a

asthma an illness which makes it difficult to take air into your body

breathe to make air move into and out of your body through your nose and mouth

nerd a person who is stupid and hasn't got many friends

length of the pool before she was twelve years old. But she loved swimming, and she didn't stop.

Slowly she became a strong and fast swimmer and in the end she could swim many lengths very well. Soon she was faster than all the children in her school. She swam for the school team and then she swam for the Colorado team. Amy said, 'One day I want to win an Olympic gold medal.'

By 1994 she was one of the ten best swimmers in the world and in 1996 she was in the American Olympic team. That year, the Olympic Games were in Atlanta, so she was very happy to swim for her country. When she won her fourth gold medal she said, 'These medals are for all of the nerds out there.'

Fanie Lombaard

STEPHANUS LOMBAARD

Fanie Lombaard, from South Africa, **broke** three **world records** in Sydney, in 2000, when he was thirty-one. He won the **pentathlon**, he **threw** the **shot** 13.75 metres, and he threw the discus 47.80 metres . . . and he did it all on one leg.

Fanie played rugby when he was younger. In 1992, he played for South Africa in a rugby game in Sydney. He broke his left leg very badly in the game and it didn't get better. When he went back home the doctors in South Africa thought it was best for him to lose the leg. Of course with only one leg he couldn't play rugby again, but he could do other sports.

Fanie wants people to call him an athlete and not a **disabled** athlete. He needs to take off and put on different legs for different sports, but says, 'Now, I've got five legs! I've got my right leg, and I've got a leg for running, a leg for the shot, a leg for the discus, and a leg for cycling.'

In 2000, Fanie cycled 1,290 kilometres from Pretoria to Cape Town to get money for disabled children. He wants young children to understand about disabled people. And he wants to help more disabled people to begin doing sport.

Magic Johnson

EARVIN JOHNSON

Magic Johnson was a great basketball player. He's over two metres tall and he played very exciting basketball when he was younger. He sometimes threw the ball to other players without looking at them, he stopped running suddenly, and he smiled a lot at the people watching on television. Everyone loved him and nobody thought there was a thing wrong with him. But now, some years later, all the world knows Magic Johnson is **HIV positive**.

Magic was born on August 14, 1959, in Michigan, with the name Earvin Johnson. His love for basketball began when he was a little boy. At seven o'clock every morning, Earvin met his friends to play basketball together before they went to school. He was very good with the ball, and at school his friends called him '**Magic**'.

After he left school, Magic went to Michigan State University, the university with the best basketball team in America. After university, in 1979, he became a professional basketball player and went to play for the Los

disabled when you can't use a part of your body well

HIV positive with the virus that can become AIDS

magic doing things that nobody can usually do

Angeles Lakers. The next year they won the National Basketball Association Championship for the first time. Magic played for the Lakers for twelve years and they won the championship four more times when he was with them.

foundation a number of people working together to help other people

Magic was one of the best basketball players in America and his life was great. But on November 7, 1991, everything changed for Magic. He learned he was HIV positive, and he stopped playing professional basketball.

Magic played basketball again, in the 'Dream Team' at the Olympic Games in Barcelona and he won a gold medal.

Magic is a survivor and these days he wants to help other people. In 1991, he began the 'Magic Johnson **Foundation**'. This tells young people about healthy living. Magic wants young people to remember something important; 'Becoming HIV positive can happen to you, too.'

29

READING CHECK

Choose the words to complete these sentences correctly.

Amy Van Dyken couldn't **(a)** *speak/run* well when she was young. She began swimming when she was **(b)** *six/twelve*. She won **(c)** *four/ten* gold medals for swimming in 1996.

Magic Johnson loved **(d)** *baseball/basketball* when he was a boy. He became famous **(e)** *before/after* he learned he was ill. He began a foundation to help young people **(f)** *play basketball/be healthy*.

Fanie Lombaard was born in **(g)** *South Africa/South America*. He lost his leg after a bad **(h)** *sports/car* accident. He broke three world records **(i)** *after/before* his accident.

WORD WORK

Find words in the footballs to complete the sentences.

a At a sports meeting in 1935, Jesse Owens b r o k e six world r _ _ _ _ _ _ in less than one hour.

b How many l _ _ _ _ _ _ of the pool can you swim?

c People with asthma can't b _ _ _ _ _ _ very well.

d You have to be good at five different sports to do the p _ _ _ _ _ _ _ _ _ _ .

e In rugby you run with the ball and t _ _ _ _ _ it to the other players.

30

f D _ _ _ _ _ _ _ _ athletes, like Fanie Lombaard, can do different sports and break world records too!

g Did you see that goal? It was m _ _ _ _ !

GUESS WHAT

The next chapter is about disabled sportsmen and women. Tick your answers.

a The Paralympic Games are for . . .
  1 ☐ children.
  2 ☐ disabled people.
  3 ☐ women.

b The Paralympic Games always happen . . .
  1 ☐ in Greece.
  2 ☐ every six years.
  3 ☐ after the Olympic Games.

c Jean Driscoll likes . . .
  1 ☐ long races.
  2 ☐ short races.
  3 ☐ swimming.

d Diana Golden finished . . . in a world skiing championship.
  1 ☐ first
  2 ☐ tenth
  3 ☐ last

e Bob Matthews trains with . . .
  1 ☐ a trainer.
  2 ☐ his friend.
  3 ☐ his dog.

The early Olympic Games

The Olympic Games began in Greece about three thousand years ago. Only men could be Olympic athletes, and they wore nothing when they ran in Olympic races. All wars stopped for the Olympics in those days. The discus and the pentathlon began in these early Olympic Games. (The **marathon** began when Greece was at war, and a soldier ran about forty-two kilometres from a town called Marathon to Athens to tell the people there about the Greeks winning the war. The soldier died soon after he arrived in Athens.) In 394 the Romans stopped the Greek Olympic Games, because they didn't like them.

In 1896, a Frenchman – Pierre de Coubertin – began the Olympic Games again. These days the Olympic Games usually happen every four years. (They did not happen in 1916, 1940, or 1944 because there were wars in these years.)

Pierre de Coubertin

The Paralympic Games are Olympic Games for disabled athletes. Fanie Lombaard, of course, is one of these disabled sportsmen. But how did the Paralympics begin?

In the 1940s Sir Ludwig Guttmann was a doctor at the Stoke Mandeville hospital in England. At the hospital there were many disabled soldiers from World War II and

marathon a 42-kilometre race

Guttmann wanted these soldiers to get better by doing sports.

In July 1948, when the Olympic Games happened in London, Guttmann asked disabled soldiers to go to a sports meeting together at Stoke Mandeville. It was all very successful, so he did it again four years later in 1952. This time disabled soldiers from Holland came too. Because he worked a lot with disabled athletes in the 1940s and 1950s, people often call Sir Ludwig Guttmann 'the father of the Paralympics'.

Sir Ludwig Guttmann

The Paralympics are younger than the Olympics, but they are getting bigger all the time. The first true Paralympic Games happened in Rome in 1960. Four hundred disabled athletes from twenty-three different countries came to these Games. At the Sydney Paralympics in 2000, there were 4,000 disabled athletes from 122 countries!

These days there are Paralympic Games every four years, and because it's easier for Paralympic athletes to stay in Olympic hotels and to run in Olympic stadiums, the Paralympics usually happen in the Olympic cities, too.

wheelchair a chair with wheels for somebody who can't walk

Think of playing basketball in a **wheelchair**. Think of skiing with only one leg. Think of running when you can't see in front of you. Disabled people can do some wonderful things! Here are the stories of three disabled athletes.

Jean Driscoll

Jean Driscoll was born in Wisconsin on November 18, 1966. Because there was something wrong with her back when she was born, she can't walk and she has a wheelchair to move about in. But she can make that wheelchair go very fast!

Jean began playing wheelchair basketball when she was a young woman. Then she went to the University of **Illinois**, and there she became interested in wheelchair racing.

She won the Boston Marathon for wheelchair athletes eight times and she is the only athlete, **able-bodied** or disabled, to do that. From 1988 to 2000 she won five gold medals in the Paralympic Games; and she came second in the 800-metres wheelchair race in the Olympic Games in 1992 and 1996.

Like Fanie Lombaard, Jean wants people to call her an athlete and not a disabled athlete. She wants people to speak well of disabled athletes for being good at their sport and not only for being disabled sportsmen and sportswomen.

Illinois /ɪlə'nɔɪ/

able-bodied not disabled; when you can use all parts of your body well

Champaign /ʃæm'peɪn/

Jean wants more disabled people to do great things too. She gives talks on television and in 2000 she wrote a book about her story. 'Dream big, and work hard,' she says to everyone. She now lives in **Champaign**, Illinois, and there is a street in Champaign called 'Jean Driscoll Lane'.

Diana Golden

Diana Golden was born in New England in the USA. She began skiing when she was a little girl and she dreamt of being a famous skier one day. Then, at the age of twelve, her right leg suddenly broke one winter day after an afternoon's skiing. In hospital the doctor looked at it carefully and then told her, 'We're afraid you have cancer in your leg, so we're going to take it off.'

A few days later, in hospital, Diana called her doctor. 'Can I ski with one leg?' she asked him. 'Of course, you can!' he said.

Two months later, Diana was skiing again. Things weren't easy for her. She was only a child after all. But she trained every day and she became very good at her sport. She won ten world championships and an Olympic gold medal for her skiing.

But the most important day of her life was in 1987. She didn't win the race that day; she came in at number ten. But it was a world championship race and she was the only disabled person competing with able-bodied skiers. Diana said, 'When I was at school children laughed at me because I had only one leg. But now I'm faster than some athletes with two legs!'

Sadly, Diana Golden could not win her fight with cancer, and she died on August 25, 2001 at the age of thirty-eight.

Bob Matthews

Bob Matthews running in the Paralympic Games, Sydney 2000

Bob Matthews is **blind**. He was born in England on May 26, 1961. Usually he works in an office, but he's a very good runner in his free time. In the Paralympic Games in Sydney 2000, he won two medals. He won a gold medal in the 10,000 metres and he came second in the 5,000 metres.

In a race, blind athletes need a **guide** who can see and help them run. In the 10,000 metres, runners have two guides. The guides must be very fast and very strong. They run together with the blind athletes and are their 'speaking eyes'. They tell them when there is someone in front of them or when they can run faster.

Bob is good at making people laugh. At the Sydney Olympics he said, 'I want to win medals in the 5,000 metres and 10,000 metres, but I'm running in the marathon only because I want to see all of Sydney cheaply!'

He says he has the healthiest guide dog in Britain. His nine-year-old dog Quando always goes running with him when he's training for a race.

blind when you can't see

guide a person (or animal) who shows or tells other people where to go

The men and women in this book – disabled and able-bodied – are only some of the true heroes of sport from different times and from different countries in the world. There are many more. Who is your favourite sports hero of yesterday or today? Where do they come from and why do you like them? And who are going to be the sports heroes of tomorrow? Perhaps they can teach us something important too.

READING CHECK

Match the first and second parts of these sentences.

a In 394 the Romans . . .

b In 1896 Pierre de Coubertin . . .

c 1n 1948 Sir Ludwig Guttmann . . .

d In 1960 the first Paralympic games . . .

e In 1966 Jean Driscoll . . .

f From 1988 to 2000 Jean . . .

g At the age of twelve Diana Golden . . .

h In 1987 Diana . . .

i Diana didn't win that race, but she . . .

j Bob Matthews . . .

k In 2000 Bob . . .

1 began the Olympic Games again.

2 happened in Rome.

3 learned she had cancer in her right leg.

4 was born in Wisconsin.

5 stopped the Greek Olympic games.

6 began the first games for disabled athletes.

7 was in a world championship race with able-bodied skiers.

8 won two medals at the Paralympics in Sydney.

9 won five gold medals for wheelchair racing in the Paralympics.

10 came in at number ten.

11 was born blind.

WORD WORK

Use words from Chapter 6 to complete the sentences.

a B l i n d people can't read with their eyes, but many of them can read with their finge
They sometimes have a g _ _ _ _ dog to help them walk through the streets.

b When disabled people can't walk, they can often use a wh _ _ _ _ _ _ _ _ to move roun

c The m _ _ _ _ _ _ _ is a long race.

activities

WHAT NEXT?

**Here are some other famous sports heroes.
Who would you like to learn more about? Why?**

IAN THORPE

CHAD ROWAN

Ian 'Thorpedo' is a swimmer from
Australia. The water in swimming pools
made him ill when he was a boy. At the
age of seventeen he won three gold
medals at the 2000 Olympics in Sydney.

Chad Rowan was born in Hawaii, USA, but
he became a famous sumo wrestler in
Japan. He is the only *yokozuna* (great
sumo champion) not to come from Japan.
His Japanese name is Akebono.

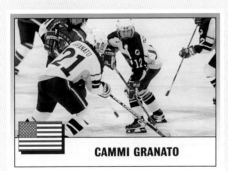

CAMMI GRANATO

ELLEN MACARTHUR

Cammi Granato is a woman ice hockey
player from the United States. Women's
ice hockey is a new Olympic sport. Cammi
got the first women's Olympic ice-hockey
goal in a match with China in 1998.

Ellen MacArthur was born in the north of
England. She got her first boat with three
years of her school dinner money. At the
age of twenty-four she sailed in a race
round the world. She finished second.

PROJECT A

MY SPORTS HERO

1 **Read the project on page 41 and answer these questions about Ellen MacArthur.**

   a When and where was she born?

   b What did she become interested in when she was a child?

   c Why wasn't it easy for her to make her dreams come true?

   d What did she do to become famous?

   e What world records does she have?

My Sports Hero

Ellen MacArthur

This is Ellen. She's my sports hero.

This is Ellen's sailing boat. It's called 'Kingfisher'.

Ellen MacArthur was born in 1976 in Derbyshire in the north of England. At the age of 8 she became interested in sailing. She put the money for her school dinners in a money box for three years and got her first boat with it.

Making her dreams come true wasn't easy for her because Derbyshire is not near the sea and she is not from a rich family. She is only 1.57 metres tall.

At the age of eighteen Ellen sailed round Britain. At the age of twenty-four she sailed round the world in the Vendée Globe Sailing race. She finished second.

She is the youngest person to finish the Vendée Globe Sailing race, and she is the fastest woman to sail round the world.

2 Make a project page about your sports hero.

PROJECT B

MY FAVOURITE SPORT

1   Look at the pictures. What sport are they playing?
    Which of these sports would you like to play?

ball
net
T-shirt
shorts
trainers
court

helmet
goal
stick
ice rink
skates
puck

42

2 **Complete the table using the words in the pictures.**

name	VOLLEYBALL	ICE HOCKEY
where	(a)	(e) ....
players	6 players	6 players
what do they wear	(b)	(f) ....
how	hit the (c) .... with hands over the (d)	hit the (g) .... with a (h) .... into the (i) ....
score	points	goals
famous championship	World Cup	Stanley Cup
opinion	fun and easy to play	the world's fastest team game, exciting to watch

3 **Read the project about ice hockey and then look at the volleyball project on page 44.**

ICE HOCKEY

My favourite sport is ice hockey. You play it on an ice rink. There are six players in a team. The players wear helmets and skates. They hit the puck with their sticks. The players must hit the puck into the other team's goal. The team with most goals wins!

The Toronto Maple Leafs are a famous team in Canada. The Stanley Cup is a famous championship in ice hockey. Ice hockey is the world's fastest team game. It is very exciting to watch!

4 Complete the project about volleyball. Use the information on pages 42–43 to help you.

VOLLEYBALL

My favourite sport is volleyball. You play it **(a)** ....
.... There are **(b)** ....
.... The players wear **(c)** ....
They hit the **(d)** .... The players
must hit the ball back to the other team. When they don't hit
the ball back they lose and the other team wins a point.

The team **(e)** .... wins!

(f) .... are a famous team in
(g) .... **(h)** ....
.... famous championship in volleyball. It happens
every four years. Volleyball is **(i)** ....
....

---

5 Make a project page about your favourite sport.